Aggregate
Economic Analysis

JOSEPH P. McKENNA
University of Missouri–St. Louis

Aggregate
Economic Analysis

third edition

THE DRYDEN PRESS INC.
HINSDALE, ILLINOIS

To **ALVIN HANSEN**
the father of us all

Preface to the Third Edition

Continuing developments in macroeconomic theory and practice have produced many amendments to the general structure of aggregate analysis. Nevertheless, the basic structure of the theory, and of this book, is substantially unchanged despite many revisions.

Like its predecessors, this edition is intended for students. I have tried, therefore, to keep the basic structure as clear as possible, so that the student will not lose sight of the goal while pursuing details. The plan of analysis begins with the simplest form, gradually working to the most complex. Each step, from the simple three-variable model of Chapter 4, through the *IS–LM* curves of Chapter 11, to the total aggregate demand and supply analysis of Chapter 13, is developed by the progressive addition of new elements. A fringe benefit of this approach is that students will come to understand the process of construction of models in economics, as well as the particular model that we use in aggregate analysis.

Many detailed changes have been made in following this plan. Chapter 4 has been simplified by removing government. Government spending, taxes, and transfers are added in Chapter 5 and kept throughout the remainder of the book. A new chapter dealing with international trade has been added. All analysis is in real terms, with prices assumed constant through Chapter 11 and variable thereafter. Algebraic derivations have been kept to a minimum, or confined to appendixes, especially in Chapters 5, 9, and 10. I have done this because I have found that, despite the increasing mathematical competence of students, there still exists a sizable group who are frightened by too much algebra, however simple it may be.

Many teachers will wish to supplement this analysis. Some will use problems, such as those in Alpha C. Chiang, *Exercises in Aggregate Economics,* second edition. Others will wish to assign additional readings, such as M. G. Mueller, *Readings in Macroeconomics.* Many economists prefer to assign the latest *Economic Report of the President* and to concentrate on policy. Another alternative is to work through one of the large models of the American economy, such as the Brookings or Office of Business Economics models. In order to facilitate this last choice, Chapter 2 has been expanded to include sectoral accounts, and appendixes have been added to Chapters 4 and 10, which deal with business saving and the role of the banks in the money supply. These additions help to explain the details of the larger models.

I am indebted to many economists, living and dead, for their contributions to macrotheory and its presentation. I am especially grateful for the comments of Belton M. Fleischer, Frederick O. Goddard, and Lawrence S. Ritter who provided critical readings of the manuscript, as well as to my University of Missouri-St. Louis colleagues John Hand and Ingo Walter. My wife performed her usual invaluable functions as draftsman, typist, and critic.

Joseph P. McKenna

University of Missouri-St. Louis
November 1968

Contents

List of Illustrations

List of Tables

Aggregate Economic Analysis

1

The Macroeconomic Approach

Economics is the study of the relation of man's wants to his resources. In the past, economics has been principally concerned with problems of choice—for example, how much labor and how much capital should be used to produce a given product. Economics has discussed many aspects of these problems of choice, but its principal focus has always been the study of individual firms and households. Most of the elementary textbooks in economics published in this century have emphasized this kind of analysis, called *microeconomics*.

In the last thirty years, a different problem has become more prominent. The theory of choice emphasizes the *direction* of expenditure or of resource use, but is little concerned with the question of *whether* the expenditure will be made at all or the resource used. This narrowness of focus stemmed from the belief that in the long run all income would be spent (either for consumption or for investment) and all resources would be employed. Consideration of the justification for such belief is beyond the scope of this book. However, it is now abundantly clear that in the short run, at least, income can be saved and not invested and resources can be unemployed. It is therefore of interest to us to consider what factors determine the short-run levels of demand and supply of total production. We shall then be in a position to discuss the level of national income, the level of prices, and the level of employment, in short, *macroeconomics.*

Before continuing, let us consider precisely what problems we hope to solve. We have said that we wish to consider total production. We might do this in at least two ways.

The first method seems perfectly straightforward. If we want to consider total production we need only consider in turn every firm and household and their outputs. Then, if we understand each of these, we shall understand total production, just as one might come to "understand" a forest by examining the plants and animals that compose it. However, the sheer magnitude of the task indicates that before we finished studying the last household, any information gleaned about the first would be obsolete. But even this understates the difficulty of the task, for it is not possible to study the elements one by one. Each unit (firm or household) is affected by other units—if not all other units, at least those nearby—as the tree in the forest is affected by those trees around it. In order to accomplish the task that we have outlined, it would be necessary to consider millions of households and thousands of firms at the same time. This task is beyond the capabilities not only of a man with pencil and paper but also of any computing machine now in existence.

The second method is more modest. It suggests that we throw away some information, thereby getting the problem down to a manageable size. Instead of considering the income of each household, we might lump all these household incomes together and discuss national income. Instead of discussing each household's purchases of meat and potatoes, we add all commodities and all households and call it consumption. We will discuss these totals in Chapter 2.

For a moment, let us remind ourselves of the questions we cannot hope to answer in this fashion. Since by this method we shall be considering only total income, we can learn nothing about why incomes are distributed in a certain way. Since we shall be considering all commodities together, we can say nothing about the relative quantities of margarine and butter sold. Many similar problems will go unanswered for the same reason. The one advantage in this method is that it enables us to discuss the totals, whereas if we insist on the complete survey called for by the first method, we may find our aspirations nobler but our accomplishments fewer.

It must not be supposed that the problems and methods discussed in this book comprise all of modern economics. Our treatment here of the selected topics constitutes little more than an introduction and leaves much to the student's future work. In particular, changes over time are discussed only briefly. Nor are the problems selected for discussion here the only important ones. The theory of choice still offers the only method of understanding many of the problems omitted and is still an important part of economics. We are here considering only an approximation method, which is adequate for some purposes. Beyond this limited scope, no claims should be made.

The discussion that makes up this book is a single unit. We could "lay out" the entire system at the outset and spend the remainder of the book justifying each part. Instead, we shall study each topic separately, adding it to the material that has gone before. In this way, we shall use the intermediate steps to build the total system.

Like many problems in economics, aggregate analysis can be divided into the study of supply and demand. Chapters 4 through 12 discuss demand, first in its simplest form and then with a gradual broadening of the view until a summary is presented of the entire market for goods and services and its relation to the money market. The early discussions assume fixed prices—that is, they explain *shifts* in the demand curve but not movements along it. Chapter 12 introduces price variations and movements along the demand curve. Chapter 13 discusses the aggregate supply. For comparison purposes, the classical or pre-Keynesian system is discussed, in a skeletal form in Chapter 3 and in an expanded version in Chapter 14. Finally, the last three chapters contain an application of the analysis to questions of public policy.

It is not possible to give final answers to any of these policy problems. Any answer has three components: the *facts* of the real world, the *analysis* of the relation between these facts, and the *value judgments* of the decision maker. This book, by necessity, concentrates on the analysis, for the facts change quite rapidly and the value judgments vary among individuals. The economist must limit himself to the analysis of problems and their alternative solutions, leaving to philosophers the choice of the best morally acceptable solution.

In the course of our discussion, we shall often use rather simple forms of mathematical formulations. Even when the form of the discussion is verbal, many of the principles will be similar to those of mathematics, for mathematics is merely one form of logic. It will therefore be useful at this point to examine the structure of this mathematical kind of analysis.

The basis of any descriptive system is a certain number of relations, or *functions*. "Function" is merely a general term for a statement that tells us the value of one number if we know the value of one or more other numbers. Thus, "John is five years older than his brother

Bob" is a verbal statement of a function. If we know how old Bob is, we can find John's age. This is a very simple function; many functions involve more than two numbers. "The population of New England is equal to the sum of the populations of Maine, New Hampshire, Vermont, Massachusetts, Rhode Island, and Connecticut" is a function relating the population of New England to six other figures, the populations of the individual states. Mathematically, functions are usually stated as equations.

For convenience, we call the components of these functions *variables*. Thus, our first function contains two variables, John's age and Bob's age. The second contains seven variables, the population of New England and that of each of the six states. The term "variable" may be a source of some confusion, since the factors which it represents may be fixed. Thus, at the moment, John's age is a fixed number. However, we do not yet know what that number is, and we must leave our imagination free to range over various possible values. If we can obtain enough relations, we shall be able to find the one set of values which will satisfy all the functions and enable us to obtain values for all the variables; that is, we can solve for all the unknowns.

Now the question arises as to how many relations would be "enough." If we know that John is five years older than Bob, how much more information—or "relations"—would we need in order to know John's age? It should be obvious that we need one more bit of information, which might be of various types. Either of the following will suffice.

$$\begin{cases} \text{Bob is } \tfrac{1}{2} \text{ John's age} \\ \text{Bob is 5 years old} \end{cases}$$

With either of these items of information, we could find that Bob is five and John is ten. Coming back to the population of New England, we need six additional pieces of information—that is, the population of each of the six states involved. We must, however, be careful about defining "additional" information. If John is five years older than Bob, the statement that Bob is five years younger than John is not additional information but merely the same thing we already know stated in a different form.

In the same way, if we are told the population of Maine, New Hampshire, Vermont, Massachusetts, and Rhode Island and the combined population of Maine and New Hampshire, we still cannot arrive at the population of New England, because, although we have six pieces of information, only five add to our knowledge. Learning the population of Maine and New Hampshire together gives us no added information if we already know the population of the two states separately.

We can therefore state as a general rule that in order to obtain a solution to any of our problems, we must have as many *independent* functions as we have variables. A system that satisfies this requirement is called a closed system, whereas a system that has fewer relations than are necessary is called an open system.

If we wish always to obtain complete answers, we can consider only closed systems. Often, however, it is useful to consider something less than a complete answer, especially as an intermediate step to a final solution. In elementary economics, it is explained that a supply curve can be derived from a set of functions covering the costs of individual factors of production, the technical production function, and the rules of profit maximization. That system of functions is not a closed system but an open one. The supply curve merely summarizes all these other relationships into one single function relating price and quantity. Only by adding another function, the demand curve, can we actually find the price and output. Nevertheless, the supply curve is useful as a device for summarizing a number of functions. In some chapters we shall discuss open systems, leaving till later a consideration of the additional information needed to close the system.

In times past, when the government played only a small part in the economic activities of this country, it was possible for economists to construct a closed system. However, the government now is a large purchaser of goods and services. The explanation for such increased government activity is beyond the competence of an economist, since it involves a large area of political decision. An open system can be made into a formally closed system simply by assigning an arbitrary function giving the value of any variable we do not wish to explain. In our first example, our statement that Bob's age is five years may be regarded as such a function; it tells Bob's age regardless of the value of the other variables. (In mathematics, this is called a function even though it is arbitrary, for it enables us to find Bob's age if we know John's age. The fact that we know Bob is five even if we know nothing of John's age is considered unimportant.) Often we shall represent such a value by an arbitrary symbol, to indicate that this variable has a value that we have no intention of explaining. We shall see, for example, that it is ordinarily possible to rearrange the information we have in such a way that any one of the other variables can be stated as a function of the variable that we are not explaining.

It is customary to call the variables we do not intend to explain "exogenous" and those that we explain "endogenous." The distinction between exogenous and endogenous variables is not a property of the real world, but merely a description of the self-imposed limitation of our analysis. In the chapters to come, we shall start with a very simple system, adding new relations and new variables in later chapters. Often variables that have been treated as exogenous in earlier chapters will be treated as endogenous in later chapters, as our analysis becomes extended.

We shall usually designate variables by capital letters. The value of an exogenous variable will be represented by the letter for that variable with a subscript zero.

In a broader sense, all economic systems are open. Unlike chemists and physicists, we do not control the environment we are studying, so we must pretend that "other things are equal." Every time the other things change, certain functions will shift. Thus all economic systems have many *unspecified exogenous variables* which are not even mentioned, in addition to the *specified exogenous variables* that are actually included in the equations. Every shift in a function can be traced to a change in one or more unspecified exogenous variables.

It may be useful to summarize the mathematical tools we shall be using. A function is represented by an equation that indicates the equality between two numbers or groups of numbers. An equation is unaffected by any change, provided that the change is made on both sides of the equation. Thus, we can add the same number to each side, subtract the same number, multiply by the same number, or divide by the same number without changing the basic statement that the equation makes. To illustrate these principles, let us use the example of the two boys' ages. We shall represent John's age by J, Bob's age by B. We then have two equations:

$$J = B + 5 \qquad (1.1)$$
$$B = \tfrac{1}{2} J \qquad (1.2)$$

To find John's age, let us insert the value of B from the second equation into the first equation. We then have

$$J = (\tfrac{1}{2} J) + 5 \qquad (1.3)$$

Subtracting $\tfrac{1}{2} J$ from each side, we obtain

$$J - \tfrac{1}{2} J = \tfrac{1}{2} J + 5 - \tfrac{1}{2} J$$
$$\tfrac{1}{2} J = 5 \qquad (1.4)$$

We then multiply both sides by 2:

$$2 \left(\tfrac{1}{2} J\right) = 2 \times 5$$
$$J = 10$$

(1.5)

To find Bob's age, we insert this value into either the first or second equations. If we use Equation 1.1 we get

$$10 = B + 5$$

(1.6)

Subtracting 5 from each side gives us

$$10 - 5 = B + 5 - 5$$
$$5 = B$$

(1.7)

For such a simple problem, these techniques may seem needlessly complicated. For later problems they will be quite useful. No more complicated mathematical tools will be required.

Another way of solving the same problem would be to draw a graph of each of the two equations, in which case the solution is found at the intersection of the two graphs. This method is exemplified in Figure 1.1.

One final problem remains. Often we group certain numbers within parentheses. When we remove the parentheses, we must multiply *each* number inside the parentheses by the number that stands in front of the parentheses. We must also watch the signs carefully. Minus times minus or plus times plus results in a plus sign; minus times plus, in a minus sign. The following examples are presented as a reminder of these rules.

$$18 + 2(6 + 2) = 18 + 12 + 4$$
$$18 + 2(8) = 34$$

(1.8)

$$18 + 2(6 - 2) = 18 + 12 - 4$$
$$18 + 2(4) = 26$$

(1.9)

$$18 - 2(6 + 2) = 18 - 12 - 4$$
$$18 - 2(8) = 2$$

(1.10)

$$18 - 2(6 - 2) = 18 - 12 + 4$$
$$18 - 2(4) = 10$$

(1.11)

When general cases are discussed in this book we shall use letters to represent numbers. The principles we have discussed above will nevertheless still apply.

Graphic Solution *of* an Equation System

FIGURE 1.1

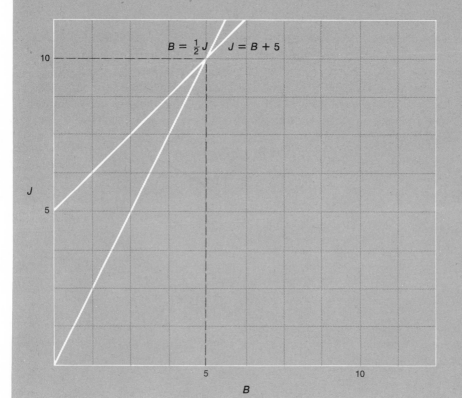

SUGGESTED ADDITIONAL READINGS

Those who are unfamiliar with the elementary mathematics discussed in this chapter will find a brief discussion in W. L. Crum and J. A. Schumpeter, *Rudimentary Mathematics for Economists and Statisticians* (New York: McGraw-Hill, 1946), Chapters 1 and 2. These chapters also contain a review of simple graphic analysis.

2

National Income and Product

Aggregate economics deals with the total activity of an economy. We must therefore pause to define measures of this activity, in order to make clear exactly what we are talking about. The definitions used here are those of the Department of Commerce, which regularly publishes national income and product statistics for the United States.

National income is the sum of the earned incomes of all individuals during a given period of time. In the United States, national income is measured on an annual basis. The sum thus determined must be distinguished from the total of cash receipts by individuals. Money withheld from wages is earned, but not included in cash receipts. The same is true of earnings retained by corporations or of wages earned but not paid, as would be the case if the end of the year fell in the middle of a work week. Gifts, either from individuals or from the government, are cash receipts but are not earned and are therefore not considered as income. Even pensions are excluded because they are not earned during the period in which they are paid.

Incomes are earned by producing goods or services. The value of production is represented by the incomes of the producers, in the form of wages, salaries, rent, interest, or profits. Thus, the total of all incomes must be identical with the value of all goods produced, for all income is generated by production and all production generates income.

National income and product are two sides of the circular flow in our economy. Households pay money to firms in exchange for the goods and services that the firms produce. Firms pay money to households in payment for the productive services that make the output possible. In reality, there are two circular flows, one of goods and services, the other of money. The money flow, national product and national income, pays for the flow of goods and services. Since goods and services are heterogeneous, consisting of food and clothing, baseball bats and lollipops, screw drivers and blast furnaces, and the assorted skills of thousands of classifications of workers, the money flow is chosen as our measure. In so doing, the market valuation of all goods is accepted rather than any other criterion. A textbook is included at the selling price, not at the higher value that its author attributes to it, nor at the lower one that some students might set. No adjustments are made for the lack of esthetic value of certain movies or records, nor for the supercleaning-power of the latest detergent unless these values are reflected in the market price.

Since national income and national product must be identical, one can measure either the income side or the product side and, in practice, usually both. In adding up production, nevertheless, one must be very careful not to count any production twice. The national product does not include the total value of steel plus the total value of automobiles because some of the steel went into the automobiles. One must, therefore, think of the national product as the total value of *additions* to the product made by the automobile industry, the steel industry, and all others. This addition—or *value added*—includes all payments made to factors of production, but excludes amounts paid to other firms. National income is thus similar to the consolidated income of a corporation and its subsidiaries.

Another way to avoid double counting is to total all final goods and services (those sold outside the business system) and to add that part of the output of steel and other intermediate goods which is not included in the value of final products. The total of final products includes all goods and services sold to consumers, to the government, and to foreign buyers. The intermediate goods that must be added are all those that go into inventories, machinery, business construction, and the like. In this manner, one excludes those sales to businesses which go into further production but includes those which add to the capital of the firm. (Readers with some background in accounting will notice that all those purchases that appear as expenses are excluded. Purchases on capital account become balance sheet items and are not counted as costs of production.)

National Income and Product Account

Table 2.1 shows the national income and product account of the United States for a recent year. This table shows a certain degree of detail. It is clear, of course, that we could use either less detail or more than that actually shown here.

On the right-hand side, the national product of the United States is shown. The national product is grouped into four main categories. The first of these is *personal consumption expenditures,* usually referred to simply as consumption. If we were interested in welfare we would want to know about the actual use of consumer goods; but for our purposes, their purchase is more important. However, the existing stocks of consumer goods are very important in analyzing current purchases. We shall return to this point in Chapter 6 when we discuss consumption in more detail.

The second component of national product is *private domestic investment.* Investment consists of purchases of plant and equipment, of new residential housing, and net change in business inventories. Two major questions arise in measuring investment. The first is whether to measure plant and equipment purchases on a *net* or a *gross* basis. Some of these purchases represent actual increases in productive capacity, but many are merely replacements for facilities that have worn out. If all purchases are included the resulting figure is called *gross investment;* if replacements are excluded the total is *net investment.* Ideally, net investment should be used because it measures the actual increase in productive capacity. Unfortunately, the only estimates available of the amount of replacement are based upon depreciation reported on income tax. This figure is certainly too high, because there is a natural bias toward overstatement in order to reduce the tax due. As a result the measurement of gross

TABLE 2.1

NATIONAL INCOME AND PRODUCT ACCOUNT, 1967

Line
1　Compensation of employees　468.2
　2　Wages and salaries　423.4
　　3　Disbursements (2 − 7)　423.4
　　4　Wage accruals less disbursements (5 − 4)　0.0
　5　Supplements to wages and salaries　44.8
　　6　Employer contributions for social insurance
　　　(3 − 14)　21.5
　　7　Other labor income (2 − 8)　23.3
8　Proprietors' income (2 − 9)　60.7
9　Rental income of persons (2 − 10)　20.3
10　Corporate profits and inventory valuation adjustment　80.4
　11　Profits before tax　81.6
　　12　Profits tax liability (3 − 11)　33.5
　　13　Profits after tax　48.1
　　　14　Dividends (2 − 11)　22.9
　　　15　Undistributed profits (5 − 5)　25.2
　16　Inventory valuation adjustment (5 − 6)　−1.2
17　Net interest (2 − 13)　23.3

18　NATIONAL INCOME　652.9

19　Business transfer payments (2 − 17)　3.1
20　Indirect business tax and nontax liability (3 − 12)　69.6
21　Less: Subsidies less current surplus of government enterprises
　　(3 − 6)　1.6
22　Statistical discrepancy (5 − 9)　−3.5
23　Capital consumption allowances (5 − 7)　69.2

CHARGES AGAINST GROSS NATIONAL PRODUCT　789.7

SOURCE: *Survey of Current Business*, July 1968, pp. 16–17.

investment has a higher degree of accuracy and is more commonly used. [The resulting national product figure is called *gross national product* (GNP).] The capital consumption allowances are given on the left side of the account as a charge against GNP. Those who wish may subtract this allowance from investment and obtain *net investment* and *net national product* (NNP). The business inventory

TABLE 2.1

NATIONAL INCOME AND PRODUCT ACCOUNT, 1967

Line
24	Personal consumption expenditures (2 − 3)				492.2
	25 Durable goods			72.6	
	26 Nondurable goods			215.8	
	27 Services			203.8	
28	Gross private domestic investment (5 − 1)				114.3
	29 Fixed investment			108.2	
		30 Nonresidential		83.6	
			31 Structures	27.9	
			32 Producers' durable equipment	55.7	
		33 Residential structures		24.6	
	34 Change in business inventories			6.1	
35	Government purchases of goods and services (3 − 1)				178.4
	36 Federal			90.6	
		37 National defense		72.4	
		38 Other		18.2	
	39 State and local			87.8	
40	Net exports of goods and services				4.8
	41 Exports (4 − 1)			45.8	
	42 Less imports (4 − 2)			41.0	

GROSS NATIONAL PRODUCT   789.7

Numbers in parenthesis show table and line of offsetting entry.

change is always shown net: that is, decreases in inventories are subtracted from increases.

The second question about investment deals with the treatment of residential housing. All purchases of new houses are treated as business investment, even though many purchases are made by consumers. The reason for this treatment is to achieve comparable treatment of owner-occupied and tenant-occupied housing. Otherwise, changes in national income could occur solely by the change in percentage of home ownership. Therefore every owner of residential property is treated as a real estate investment firm. Rental payments and imputed rents are treated as personal consumption expenditures. Any "profits" on owning one's own home are added into total income. Thus the sale of a house by a real estate firm to an individual who occupies it would not change the national income and product accounts. This treatment is different from that used for other consumer durable goods, which are considered consumed when purchased. The reasons are that other durables have shorter lives and that no significant rental market exists. If automobile leasing should grow in significance in the future, it is probable that automobiles may be given similar treatment.

The third component of the national product is *government purchases of goods and services*. Unlike private accounting, government accounts do not distinguish between current expenses and capital assets. All expenditures are treated the same, whether they are the wages of a government employee or the cost of a new building. Periodically, it is proposed that government accounts should make special allowance for capital (and depreciation), but the change has never been made.

The final part of national product is *net exports*. Some of our total output is not destined for domestic use, either by consumers, investors, or government. These exports must therefore be added to the total product. However, some portion of the domestic demand for consumption, investment, and government purchases is satisfied by imported goods. Therefore we add exports and subtract imports to obtain the total national product.

On the left side of the accounts are national income and other charges against GNP. National income includes all incomes earned, even those which are not paid out to the earners. It includes wages, rent, interest, and profit; but also social security payments, corporate profits taxes, and retained corporate earnings. (One item, *inventory valuation adjustment*, may need some explanation. This is an adjustment to profits to correct for changes in the prices at which inventory is carried.)

Of the other charges against GNP, we have already discussed capital consumption allowances. *Business taxes* and *business transfers* are items that are included in the selling price of goods but not in the earnings of factors. Thus national income is NNP measured at factor cost, and NNP is national income measured at product prices.

In principle, one should be able to measure the economic activity of a country either from the income side or the product side. Unfortunately, our statistical materials are not of sufficient accuracy to cause these two measurements to come out evenly. The *statistical discrepancy* is the "fudge factor" required to produce a balance. (It is not a measure of the accuracy of the national accounts. It is quite possible that both sides may be in error in the same direction.)

Sector Accounts

To display the interrelationships of the economy, a set of sector accounts are used, for households, government, and foreign transactions. (Before 1954 a separate business account was used, but it has been abandoned, largely on the ground that it was more confusing than helpful.) These sector accounts are shown as Tables 2.2, 2.3, and 2.4. Each of them contains the offsetting items of the national income and product account plus certain other items that are treated as income by the sector but to which no product is attached. These flows are called *transfer payments*. The largest of them is *government transfer to persons*. This transfer represents payments (of relief, pensions, and so forth) for which no matching flow of services is received. Other transfers include government and personal transfers to foreigners and business transfers to persons.

The right-hand side of the personal income and outlay account contains all the income items of the national income and product account except for taxes and retained earnings. In addition, it includes transfers from business and government. In a somewhat dubious decision, the U.S. Department of Commerce chose to treat interest paid by government and by consumers as a transfer payment on the ground that no identifiable service was attached. (Business interest is still treated as earned income.)

On the left side are the uses of income. These include taxes, personal outlays, and saving. Since consumers have little control over taxes but substantial control over the other uses, it is useful to subtract personal taxes from personal income to obtain *disposable income*. This latter amount can then be allocated by consumers either to consump-

TABLE 2.2

PERSONAL INCOME AND OUTLAY ACCOUNT, 1967

Line

1 Personal tax and nontax payments (3 − 10)		82.5
2 Personal outlays		506.2
3 Personal consumption expenditures (1 − 24)	492.2	
4 Interest paid by consumers (2 − 15)	13.1	
5 Personal transfer payments to foreigners (net) (4 − 4)	0.8	
6 Personal saving (5 − 3)		40.2

PERSONAL TAXES, OUTLAYS, AND SAVING   628.8

SOURCE: *Survey of Current Business*, July 1968, pp. 16–17.

TABLE 2.3

GOVERNMENT RECEIPTS AND EXPENDITURES
ACCOUNT, 1967

Line

1 Purchases of goods and services (1 − 35)		178.4
2 Transfer payments		50.8
3 To persons (2 − 18)	48.6	
4 To foreigners (net) (4 − 3)	2.2	
5 Net interest paid (2 − 14)		10.5
6 Subsidies less current surplus of government enterprises (1 − 21)		1.6
7 Surplus (+) or deficit (−), (5 − 8)		−13.8
8 Federal	−12.4	
9 State and local	− 1.4	

GOVERNMENT EXPENDITURES AND SURPLUS   227.4

SOURCE: *Survey of Current Business*, July 1968, pp. 16–17.

TABLE 2.2

PERSONAL INCOME AND OUTLAY ACCOUNT, 1967

Line
7	Wage and salary disbursements $(1 - 3)$		423.4
8	Other labor income $(1 - 7)$		23.3
9	Proprietors' income $(1 - 8)$		60.7
10	Rental income of persons $(1 - 9)$		20.3
11	Dividends $(1 - 14)$		22.9
12	Personal interest income		46.8
	13	Net interest $(1 - 17)$	23.3
	14	Net interest paid by government $(3 - 5)$	10.5
	15	Interest paid by consumers $(2 - 4)$	13.1
16	Transfer payments to persons		51.7
	17	From business $(1 - 19)$	3.1
	18	From government $(3 - 3)$	48.6
19	Less: Personal contributions for social insurance $(3 - 15)$		20.4

PERSONAL INCOME   628.8

TABLE 2.3

GOVERNMENT RECEIPTS AND EXPENDITURES
ACCOUNT, 1967

Line
10	Personal tax and nontax payments $(2 - 1)$		82.5
11	Corporate profits tax liability $(1 - 12)$		33.5
12	Indirect business tax and nontax liability $(1 - 20)$		69.6
13	Contributions for social insurance		41.9
	14	Employer $(1 - 6)$	21.5
	15	Personal $(2 - 19)$	20.4

GOVERNMENT RECEIPTS   227.4

TABLE 2.4

FOREIGN TRANSACTIONS ACCOUNT, 1967

Line
1   Export of goods and services (1 − 41)   45.8

RECEIPTS FROM FOREIGNERS   45.8

SOURCE: *Survey of Current Business*, July 1968, pp. 16–17.

tion or to saving. Table 2.3 represents the receipts and outlay of governments (federal, state, and local); Table 2.4 represents payments to, and receipts from, foreigners.

Saving and Investment Account

Most of the items in the accounts represent simple flows, that is, they are payments by one sector and receipts by another. Some items are not of this type. Earnings retained by business, saving of consumers, and surpluses of governments represent uses of funds by one sector, but not sources to another. In a similar sense, investment represents a product (a receipt of money), but financing does not come from current receipts of any sector. To complete the formal balance, a separate saving and investment account is established, shown in Table 2.5.

This account is not really a sector, but represents a particular type of transaction. On the right-hand side are all forms of saving—personal saving, retained profits, depreciation allowances, and government surplus. (The statistical discrepancy also appears here because it has

TABLE 2.4

FOREIGN TRANSACTIONS ACCOUNT, 1967

Line		
2	Imports of goods and services (1 − 42)	41.0
3	Transfer payments from U.S. government to foreigners (net) (3 − 4)	2.2
4	Personal transfer payments to foreigners (net) (2 − 5)	0.8
5	Net foreign investment (5 − 2)	1.7
	PAYMENTS TO FOREIGNERS	45.8

no matching transaction.) On the left are the uses of saving: domestic and foreign investment.

This account, like all the others, must balance. Its balance is a consequence of the balance in the other accounts. If all the other accounts were added together and all duplications on both sides of the account removed, the saving and investment items would remain and still be, balanced. Every dollar of income comes from a dollar of product; every dollar not spent for consumption or government (that is, every dollar saved) must come from a product other than consumption or government (that is, from investment).

Real Income and Money Income

All the money flows that we have been discussing are measured in money terms. There is no alternative method of measurement, for each flow represents a sum of payments for a large number of heterogeneous items. Only the money payments involved give a common measuring stick for these discrete items. This measuring stick has a number of disadvantages, the greatest of which is that it changes size from year to year. If one hears that national income has risen

TABLE 2.5

GROSS SAVING AND INVESTMENT ACCOUNT, 1967

Line		
1	Gross private domestic investment (1 − 28)	114.3
2	Net foreign investment (4 − 5)	1.7

GROSS INVESTMENT	116.0

SOURCE: *Survey of Current Business*, July 1968, pp. 16–17.

since last year, one cannot be sure whether more goods and services have been produced or whether the measuring stick has changed in size. In most cases there is a combination of both: a change in production *and* a change in prices. As a device to measure the change in production, the money national income is divided by the price index. For example, national income was $100 billion in 1940 and $360 billion in 1954. However, prices had doubled during the period, so it is said that national income in 1954 was $180 billion measured in 1940 dollars. Such a computation shows that 80 percent more goods and services were produced in 1954 than in 1940. This bundle of goods and services is called the *real income,* whereas, the money value is called *money income.*

The measurement of real income here is not a precise one; the constant addition of new products and changes in the quality of old ones make it impossible to obtain any exact comparisons. But even the approximate figures obtained are better than figures that disregard any difference between money income and real income.

The Department of Commerce uses a special device to adjust its figures for price change which is much more accurate than the one suggested above. A price index is prepared for every component of the national accounts. Each of these components is then adjusted to give the value of that component in constant dollars, and they are added to produce GNP in constant dollars. The department can then obtain a kind of price index by dividing the current dollar figures

TABLE 2.5

GROSS SAVING AND INVESTMENT ACCOUNT, 1967

Line		
3	Personal saving $(2 - 6)$	40.2
4	Wage accruals less disbursements $(1 - 4)$	0.0
5	Undistributed corporate profits $(1 - 15)$	25.2
6	Corporate inventory valuation adjustment $(1 - 16)$	-1.2
7	Capital consumption allowances $(1 - 23)$	69.2
8	Government surplus or deficit $(-)$ $(3 - 7)$	-13.8
9	Statistical discrepancy $(1 - 22)$	-3.5
GROSS SAVING AND STATISTICAL DISCREPANCY		116.0

by the constant dollar figures. This method is better than dividing by any one index because the importance of different components changes in time; any total index could not reflect this shifting importance, but would be forced to settle for a single set of weights. Figure 2.1 shows GNP since 1929 with the deflated (adjusted) figures and the deflator (the price index). It can readily be seen that prices have generally risen, but GNP has risen faster: consequently, the *real* GNP has risen generally.

Stocks and Flows

All of the national income and product figures measure flows: the amount of money which changes hands during a period of time. These flows are the proper way to measure the activity of a society. Sometimes, however, we might be interested in the state of an economy, in which case we would need to know the stock of assets at a given time. (Individual businesses usually publish two reports, an income statement which deals with flows and a balance sheet which deals with stocks.) No general data on stocks of our society are available;

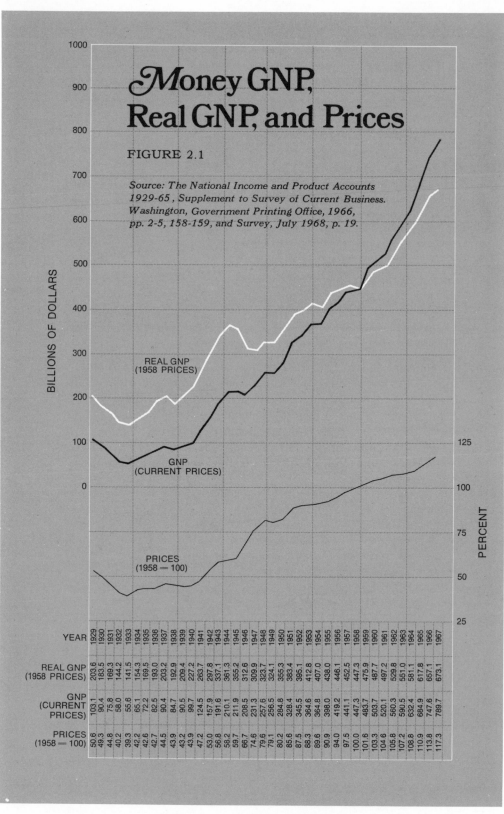

Money GNP, Real GNP, and Prices

FIGURE 2.1

Source: The National Income and Product Accounts 1929-65, Supplement to Survey of Current Business. Washington, Government Printing Office, 1966, pp. 2-5, 158-159, and Survey, July 1968, p. 19.

REAL GNP
(1958 PRICES)

GNP
(CURRENT PRICES)

PRICES
(1958 = 100)

BILLIONS OF DOLLARS

PERCENT

YEAR	REAL GNP (1958 PRICES)	GNP (CURRENT PRICES)	PRICES (1958 = 100)
1929	203.6	103.1	50.6
1930	183.5	90.4	49.3
1931	169.3	75.8	44.8
1932	144.2	58.0	40.2
1933	141.5	55.6	39.3
1934	154.3	65.1	42.2
1935	169.5	72.2	42.6
1936	193.0	82.5	42.7
1937	203.2	90.4	44.5
1938	192.9	84.7	43.9
1939	209.4	90.5	43.2
1940	227.2	99.7	43.9
1941	263.7	124.5	47.2
1942	297.8	157.9	53.0
1943	337.1	191.6	56.8
1944	361.3	210.1	58.2
1945	355.2	211.9	59.7
1946	312.6	208.5	66.7
1947	309.9	231.3	74.6
1948	323.7	257.6	79.6
1949	324.1	256.5	79.1
1950	355.3	284.8	80.2
1951	383.4	328.4	85.6
1952	395.1	345.5	87.5
1953	412.8	364.6	88.3
1954	407.0	364.8	89.6
1955	438.0	398.0	90.9
1956	446.1	419.2	94.0
1957	452.5	441.1	97.5
1958	447.3	447.3	100.0
1959	475.9	483.7	101.6
1960	487.7	503.7	103.3
1961	497.2	520.1	104.6
1962	529.8	560.3	105.8
1963	551.0	590.5	107.2
1964	581.1	632.4	108.8
1965	617.8	684.9	110.9
1966	657.1	747.6	113.8
1967	673.1	789.7	117.3

however, we are sometimes concerned with these stocks and the way they affect income flows. For example, each year's *net investment* (a flow) adds to the total *capital* (a stock). One especially confusing distinction is between *saving* (the flow representing income not consumed) and *savings* (the stock of assets which consumers acquire as the result of saving). Because of the confusion, we will avoid the term *savings* in this book and simply refer to consumer liquid assets.

We shall also need to distinguish later between *income* (the flow) and *money* (the stock that consumers and businesses hold). Every consumer must have income, but most could get by with a very small stock of money. We shall return to this point in the next chapter.

This book is primarily concerned with flows. However, at various places we will refer to stocks as a factor influencing behavior. These references are especially frequent in Chapters 6, 7, and 10. The distinction must be kept continually in mind.

cAbbreviations

Throughout this book, we shall refer to the various components of national income, sometimes in mathematical form. The following abbreviations have been adopted for the sake of convenience:

$$Y = \text{Income}$$
$$Y_D = \text{Disposable income}$$
$$C = \text{Consumption}$$
$$S = \text{Saving}$$
$$I = \text{Investment}$$
$$Tx = \text{Taxes}$$
$$Tr = \text{Transfers}$$
$$G = \text{Government expenditures}$$

Unless specifically noted otherwise, it will be assumed that all are measured in real terms.

PROBLEMS AND DISCUSSION QUESTIONS

1. If a firm manufactures materials for another firm but gives them away free, what problems would this raise in measuring national income?

2. Does paying off debts constitute saving? Why?

3. If the purchase of automobiles is treated as investment instead of as consumption, what difference would it make in the accounts in the year the automobile is purchased? In the years it is used?

4. Relief payments are treated as transfer payments; wages, as government expenditures and income. How would you classify payments made by the government to otherwise unemployed workers hired to do useless work?

5. In 1939, prices were 60 percent of the 1947 level; in 1953, they were 120 percent. GNP in current dollars was $91 billion in 1939, $234 billion in 1947, and $365 billion in 1953. Compare the real GNP in these three years.

6. Which of the measures given in Table 2.1 do you consider the best criterion of a country's economic welfare?

7. Using the data contained in the latest *Economic Report of the President*, reconstruct the sector accounts for last year.

SUGGESTED ADDITIONAL READINGS

The regular national accounts for the United States are prepared by the U.S. Department of Commerce and are issued annually, usually in the July issue of *Survey of Current Business*. Quarterly estimates of most components of the accounts are also published in the *Survey* throughout the year. Preliminary data are also published in the *Economic Report of the President* in January. Detailed statistics are collected in *The National Income and Product Accounts of the United States, 1919–65*, a supplement to the *Survey of Current Business* (1966). Detailed discussions of methodology are contained in *U.S. Income and Output* (1958) and in the August 1965 issue of the *Survey*. A comprehensive explanation of conceptual framework and statistical sources is promised for the future.

For earlier periods the best estimates are those prepared by Simon Kuznets for the National Bureau of Economic Research, a private organization. The estimates are summarized in Kuznets, *National Income: A Summary of Findings* (1946); and details of the earlier estimates are given in Kuznets, *National Product since 1869* (1946). The problem of properly defining national income is treated at length in the first three chapters of Kuznets, *National Income 1919–1938* (1941). All three books are published for the National Bureau by Princeton University Press.

A Critique of the United States Income and Product Accounts (1958) reports the proceedings of a conference sponsored by the National Bureau providing detailed discussion of the logic and the techniques of measurement. It is Number 22 in the series *Studies in Income and Wealth*, all of which are relevant to the subject. All are published by Princeton University Press.

3

The Classical System

Before 1936 when Keynes wrote *The General Theory,* the typical explanation of aggregate economic phenomena was based upon what is now called "classical" economics. This system had been refined by a number of additions to the basic analysis developed a century earlier by David Ricardo. In its essential characteristics, it was a direct outgrowth of classical price theory, the analysis of price and output behavior of firms. The theory of aggregate supply was quite sophisticated and forms the principal basis for much of modern aggregate supply theory (see Chapter 13). Its aggregate demand theory was much less adequate, and it was against this theory that Keynes directed his major attack, stressing his own theory of "effective demand." Because so much of modern theory constitutes a reaction to the classical system, it is worthwhile to pause here before looking at the later theory.

The brief picture of the classical system which follows is somewhat unfair to its exponents, who include many intellectual giants. Only the skeleton will be examined here, in order to portray the essentials of the system. In the simplified form given here, it never represented the view of any economist, but its outline was common to most of them. A more elaborate version will follow in Chapter 14.

cAggregate Supply

In the simplest form, classical aggregate supply relied on Say's law of markets, which held that general overproduction is impossible. The argument for Say's law was often given in terms of a barter economy: every unit of supply is automatically a unit of demand. It would of course be possible for the supply of any particular good to be excessive, but since each good is supplied only because the supplier wants another good in exchange, total demand and supply must be equal.

In a money economy the process is more complex, but the result is the same. People will work only if the goods which they can buy with their wages compensate them adequately for their efforts. Consequently, there would be no supply unless there is a demand for goods of equal value.

This result is a natural outgrowth of classical price theory, in which everything depends upon relative prices. Firms hire workers if their product, multiplied by the price of the product, exceeds the wage. Thus it is the ratio of product prices to wages which matters, not the absolute level of either. Similarly, a household's decision to supply labor depends upon the ratio of wages to the prices of the goods that can be bought with them. Thus aggregate supply would be independent of the absolute level of prices. It would therefore be a vertical line, as shown in Figure 3.1.

The level of output represented by the aggregate supply would depend upon conditions in the labor market. The demand for labor would be a downward sloping curve depending upon the marginal productivity of labor, but measured in terms of real wages: that is, the ratio of money wages to prices. Similarly, the supply of labor would be measured in the same terms and would depend on the households' preference for goods and aversion to work. The labor market equilibrium is shown in Figure 3.2. The intersection of the labor supply and demand curves can be called full employment, since there would be no unemployed workers seeking work. (There might be voluntarily unemployed workers who prefer to remain idle rather than accept the available work.) If the level of employment is determined by the labor supply, the technological conditions of the society would determine the amount of output that can be produced. Thus the level of the aggregate supply curve would be determined.

If there were any unemployment, it could exist only because the real wage were too high. Such a condition could not persist, since unem-

The Classical Supply Curve

FIGURE 3.1

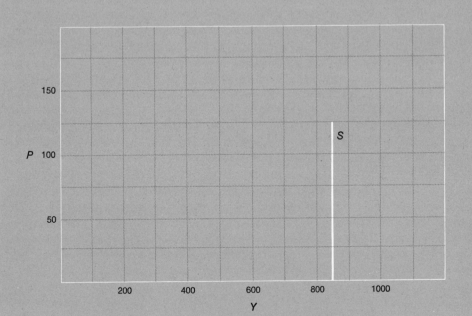

The Classical Labor Market

FIGURE 3.2

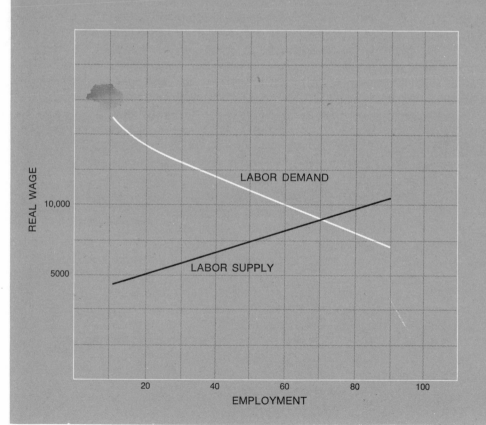

ployed workers would offer their services for lower wages, preferring low wages to none. Thus normal competition would remove unemployment just as it removes the excess supply of any commodity or service.

cAggregate Demand

The basis of classical aggregate demand is the *equation of exchange*. This equation appears in many forms but one common form is

$$MV = PY \tag{3.1}$$

Here M is the quantity of money; V its velocity; P the general price level; and Y the real income. This equation is an identity, since it states that the value of national income, PY, must be paid for with the available money, M. The velocity, V, shows us how many times per year this money must actually change hands in order to do the job. Equation 3.1 may therefore be considered merely a definition of velocity.

From the equation of exchange developed the *quantity theory of money*. The quantity theory holds that velocity is relatively constant in a society, depending upon the payment habits and financial institutions. For example, if everyone were paid monthly and spent all his income during the month, the velocity of money would be 12 times per year. The amount of money required in the society would be just enough to pay monthly wages (and profits, rents, and interest). During the month, the money would be spent, thus returning to firms in time to pay the next month's incomes. Actually a real society is more complex, and one has to allow extra time for interfirm transactions before the money could become income again. In such a case, the annual income velocity would be less than 12.

If V is relatively constant, one can obtain various relationships between the remaining three variables. For example, if the money supply is constant, prices and output would vary inversely. The aggregate demand curve would be a hyperbola, as shown in Figure 3.3.

One could also look at the same argument from the other direction. If Y is determined by the full employment level, as in Figure 3.1, then prices will always move proportionately with the money supply.

The Classical Demand Curve

FIGURE 3.3

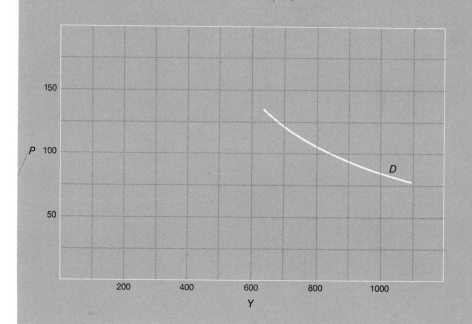

Changes in monetary actions would cause inflation and deflation (changes in prices) but not changes in output.

How did the quantity theory work in the economy? Here, a distinction must be made. With some would-be economists and popular writers, the equation of exchange was a form of mystic numerology. No explanation was required; the equation itself was sufficient. Another explanation, not much better, implied that money burns holes in people's pockets. Since money would be sought only for spending, consumers would naturally wish to increase their spending any time more money came into their hands.

Needless to say, such explanations were not adequate for good economists. They needed an explanation that was solidly based on the behavior of rational people. Such an explanation was found in the mechanism of saving and investment.

Consumers do not always wish to spend all their receipts on consumption; a part of their income will be saved. However, it would seem pointless to hold money when one could purchase bonds, stocks, or other income-producing assets. The purchase of such securities would raise their price, thereby lowering the effective rate of interest on them. (To take a simple example, if one pays $100 for a bond that will be redeemed in one year for $106, the rate of interest is 6 percent; if one pays $102, the rate of interest is only 4 percent.) The lowered rate of interest would encourage more firms to borrow and invest. This process would continue until all saving had found an outlet in new investment. The rate of interest would always adjust so that any money not spent for consumption would find its way into investment. The tendency to spend all money available has been explained in terms of "rational" consumer behavior.

Later additions to the quantity theory recognized that stocks of monetary assets often directly affect behavior. For example, consumers might be willing to consume more of their current income if their assets were higher. Such effects would reinforce the interest-rate effect discussed above.

The classical system can thus be seen to be two essentially independent processes, each of which is dependent upon a critical assumption. The determination of output depends upon real factors, the supply of labor and the technical process of production. All adjustments depend upon relative prices. The critical assumption is that prices and wages are completely free to move so that the appropriate relationships can be established.

The determination of the general price level depends upon the money supply. The price adjustment works through interest-rate adjustments and simultaneously determines the division of total demand into consumption and investment. Here the critical assumption is that all money is spent, either for consumer goods or for investment. The possibility of money-holding as rational behavior is specifically denied.

A detailed discussion of the supply system is contained in Chapter 13 and a further analysis of classical demand is given in Chapter 14. A few examples here will serve to illustrate the process of adjustment envisioned by the classical economists.

First, let us consider an increase in the money supply. Such an increase would probably come about by increased bank loans to business, thereby increasing demand deposits that would be used for investment spending. The investment spending in turn would generate consumer incomes and lead to additional consumption spending. Since both consumption and investment cannot rise if resources are fully employed, prices will rise. The increased prices would make it profitable for firms to hire more workers. Since workers are already fully employed, the increased demand will drive wages up until they have risen proportionately with prices. At this stage, equilibrium would be established again. Since the price-wage ratio is unchanged, total output will be unchanged.

As a second example, let us consider an increase in labor productivity, so that output per worker is increased. This increase would lead firms to try to hire more workers. However, the additional total product could be sold only if prices were lowered. The ratio of wages to prices therefore rises, but does not produce unemployment because of the new higher productivity. Total income would remain unchanged, with a decline in prices matched by a rise in real output.

As a last example, let us imagine an increase in the supply of labor. The immediate effect would be unemployment. Competition among workers would drive wages down, so that employers would want to hire more of them and produce more goods. These increased goods could be sold only at lower prices, so prices would fall. However, the decline in prices would be less than in wages; otherwise the old wage-price ratio would be established and unemployment would remain. A new equilibrium is established with lower prices, still lower wages, and increased output.

This last example shows why unemployment is impossible within the classical system. Flexible wages and prices would always permit adjustment so that equilibrium could be established. (There would probably be some temporary difficulty, as falling prices create expectations of further declines. Nevertheless, a new equilibrium would ultimately be established.) Consequently, if unemployment is observed to persist in the real world, it could be said that it was because the rules of the game had been broken. In particular, wages (and many other prices) are often inflexible in a downward direction. Thus, it is often possible that some fluctuation may occur (for example, in the money supply) which would lead to lower prices. If wages are flexible they will fall and produce a new equilibrium; if they are rigid unemployment results.

Some people are satisfied with this result. Any unemployment thus can be blamed on workers, or their unions which choose to hold wages up. Such a solution is unsatisfying to government administrators and to economists. To the administrator, finding someone to blame is far less important than finding a way to cure the situation. To the economist, it is not enough to analyze what the system would do if it were perfectly competitive; it is necessary to know what it will do if it is not. (After all, the purpose of a model is to help us understand the world. It is not the purpose of the world to conform to the model.) New tools of analysis were needed which would give some clue to curing depressions. Keynesian analysis was a response to this demand.

SUGGESTED ADDITIONAL READINGS

The classical theory, representing the generally accepted analysis, appeared in almost all standard textbooks published before 1936. A convenient summary may be found in Alvin Hansen, *A Guide to Keynes* (New York: McGraw-Hill, 1953), pp. 3–35.

4

The Keynesian System

Whatever its value as a general description of the economic process, the classical system was unsuitable as a guide to public affairs. The world-wide depression of the 1930s demonstrated that large-scale unemployment could continue for an extended period. To many economists, it seemed more useful to use a theory based upon shifts in a demand curve along a horizontal supply curve. The level of national product would then depend upon *shifts* in the demand curve, rather than movements along it.

In this book we shall follow this pattern. Until Chapter 12 we shall assume that the supply curve is fixed and horizontal so that prices remain constant. We shall then concentrate on those factors that alter the demand curve.

Let us start with a very simple economy in which there are only consumers and businesses, but no government. For the sake of further simplicity, let us assume that businesses do no saving, but pass on all earnings to consumers. In this case, net national product, national income, personal income, and disposable income would all be equal. We will further assume that investment is already determined by factors that are outside our present analysis. (Each of these simplifying assumptions will be removed in later chapters.)

The list of variables and the three basic equations are given below. The first equation is a definition, defining income and product as the sum of consumer sales and investment. The third equation is merely a formal way of stating that investment is exogenous and not discussed in this system. Equation 4.2, the consumption function, is defined below.

VARIABLES

Endogenous:

Y = National Income
C = Consumer Expenditures

Exogenous:

I = Investment Expenditures

EQUATIONS

$$Y = C + I \qquad (4.1)$$
$$C = a + bY \qquad (4.2)$$
$$I = I_0 \qquad (4.3)$$

All prices are assumed constant.

The Consumption Function

There are several reasons for describing consumption in the manner indicated in Equation 4.2. It is a common observation that as an individual's income increases he usually spends a part of the increase for consumption and saves a part. Therefore, the ratio of the increase in consumption expenditure to the increase in income is ordinarily between zero and one. (We might imagine some individuals who would react in a perverse fashion, but they would not be typical.) We are not so much interested in individual behavior as in the behavior of the whole society, but, in this case, the same principles that apply to individuals will apply to the society. An increase in national income will mean increases in income for some individuals. Since most of them will save some and consume some, it is reasonable to assume that the same relationship between income and consumption exists for the society as a whole; this relationship is usually designated as the *consumption function*.

Many attempts have been made statistically to find the precise form of this relationship. These studies indicate that many factors in addition to income affect the level of consumption. Such refinements are discussed in Chapter 6, together with some of the statistical results. As a first approximation, we shall ignore these other variables and discuss only the relation between income and consumption.

A few words are necessary to justify the form of relationship which we have chosen to discuss. In many cases, it would be convenient to assume that every dollar of increase in income is reflected in an equal increase in consumption—to assume, that is, that if an increase in income of $100 causes an increase of $80 in consumption, an increase in income of $1000 would cause an increase in consumption of $800, not $750 or $900. As we shall see in Chapter 6, we have reason to believe that the real world is not quite so simple; however, if we make the assumption that the increase is proportionately the same for all levels of income and confine our discussion to a fairly narrow range of incomes, any error we make will be fairly small. Thus, if an increase in income of $100 causes an increase of $80 in consumption, we should expect an additional increase of $100 in income to cause an additional increase in consumption of about $80, although it might actually be $78 or $82. In any case, the error in assuming it to be $80 would be small.

The form of equation we have chosen (a straight line) embodies this assumption that every addition to income involves a constant addition to consumption. Let us represent an increase in consumption by ΔC and an increase in income by ΔY. If income increases from Y to $Y + \Delta Y$, consumption will increase from C to $C + \Delta C$. Using Equation 4.2, we find that

$$C + \Delta C = a + b(Y + \Delta Y)$$
$$= a + bY + b\Delta Y \tag{4.4}$$

Subtracting Equation 4.2,

$$\Delta C = b\Delta Y \tag{4.5}$$

The letter b represents the portion of *additional* income that will be consumed. This proportionality factor is called the *marginal pro-*

pensity to consume. It is called marginal because it applies only to additions to income.

We can draw a graph of the consumption function, as shown in Figure 4.1. The marginal propensity to consume can be measured by drawing a triangle with sides parallel to the axes (base lines), using the consumption function as the hypotenuse. The marginal propensity to consume is then the ratio of ΔC to ΔY. For the straight-line equation that we have chosen, it is apparent that this ratio is the same regardless of the size and position of the triangle.

We might also, on occasion, be interested in the average propensity to consume, or the proportion of the average dollar which is consumed—that is, the ratio of C to Y. In Figure 4.1, we represent this ratio by drawing a line to the zero point, then using this line as the hypotenuse of a triangle. We can then measure C parallel to the vertical axis and Y along the horizontal axis. For the equation we have chosen, this ratio, unlike the marginal propensity, is not a constant but is different at every level of income. When income is low, the ratio will be more than 1, indicating that people spend more than their incomes for consumption. At high incomes, the average propensity is smaller, indicating that people do not spend all their incomes but instead save some. Table 4.1 gives a hypothetical value

TABLE 4.1

HYPOTHETICAL CONSUMPTION FUNCTION
(UNIT: $1 BILLION)

Income ($)	Consumption	Average Propensity to Consume	Marginal Propensity to Consume
0	160		0.60
100	220	2.20	0.60
200	280	1.40	0.60
300	340	1.13	0.60
400	400	1.00	0.60
500	460	0.92	0.60
600	520	0.87	0.60
700	580	0.83	0.60
800	640	0.80	0.60
900	700	0.78	0.60
1000	760	0.76	0.60

The Consumption Function

FIGURE 4.1

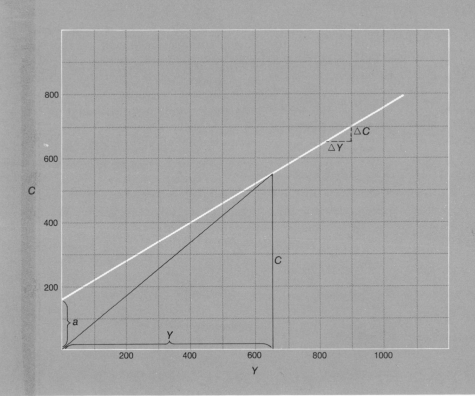

of the consumption function and the average and marginal propensities to consume.

As can be seen from Figure 4.1, a is the value of consumption when income is zero. Using the numerical example of Table 4.1, a is \$160 billion. However, one should not attach special importance to this factor. Our argument for using a straight line was that it would give us a reasonably accurate description of the consumption function in the neighborhood of equilibrium income. Clearly, the zero income level is not in that neighborhood. Therefore, a should be regarded as the constant that determines the level of the consumption function and b as the constant that determines its slope. An increase in a means that the whole line moves upward parallel to its present position; an increase in b means that the line becomes steeper.

Equilibrium Income

We are now prepared to consider the solution to this system of equations, to find the level of national income which will satisfy these conditions. We call such a level the *equilibrium* income, since there would be no tendency to move from this position, once it is attained, unless conditions change. We are not explaining the level of investment; therefore, the most we can hope for is a formal solution that illustrates the dependence of the equilibrium income upon investment. To find such a solution, let us recall the definition of Equation 4.1:

$$Y = C + I \tag{4.1}$$

We now substitute in the right-hand side of this equation the values of C and I given by Equations 4.2 and 4.3, respectively. We then obtain

$$Y = (a + bY) + I_0 \tag{4.6}$$

Subtracting bY from both sides

$$Y - bY = a + I_0 \tag{4.7}$$

We now divide by $(1 - b)$ and obtain

$$Y = \frac{1}{1 - b}(a + I_0) \tag{4.8}$$

This solution tells us the level of national income we could expect if we knew I_0 and had the numerical values of a and b. For those who prefer arithmetical solutions, this technique is indicated in Table 4.2. We have used the consumption function of Table 4.1 and assumed I_0 to be $200 billion.

In Table 4.2, the equilibrium level is 900. Only at this level would the sum of investment plus the consumption appropriate to that level add up to the total of national income.

A graphic illustration of this solution technique is presented in Figure 4.2. We have here taken the graph of the consumption function shown in Figure 4.1 and added to it the level of investment. This new line, $C + I_0$, corresponds to the last column of Table 4.2. The equilibrium value is located at the point at which this sum equals income. Since income is measured on the horizontal scale and the expenditures on the vertical scale, it is useful to extend income vertically. This is done by adding a line at a 45° angle upward, the $Y = Y$ line. The equilibrium income is then the point at which the 45° line crosses the $C + I_0$ line, or the point at which $Y = C + I_0$. As in the table, this value is $900 billion.

A study of Table 4.2 gives us also some understanding of the process by which the economy reaches the equilibrium value. In Chapter 2 we noted that firms were completely neutral in our economy, since all the income received by firms is in turn allocated to consumers.

TABLE 4.2

HYPOTHETICAL INCOME DATA
(UNIT: $1 BILLION)

Y	C	I_0	$C + I_0$
0	160	200	360
100	220	200	420
200	280	200	480
300	340	200	540
400	400	200	600
500	460	200	660
600	520	200	720
700	580	200	780
800	640	200	840
900	700	200	900
1000	760	200	960

The Equilibrium Income

FIGURE 4.2

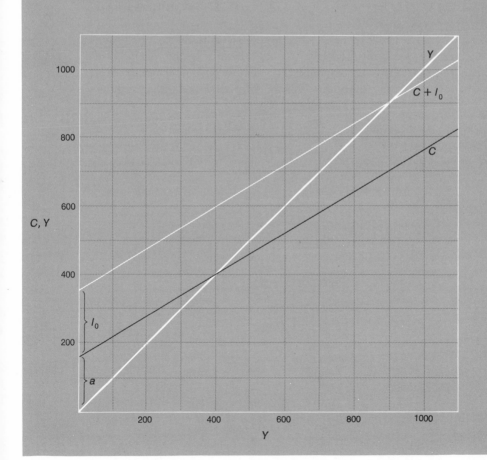

Suppose that consumers expected an income of $800 billion. They would spend $640 billion for consumption. This sum, together with $200 billion of investment, would mean $840 billion of income to firms and, in turn, to consumers. These consumers would therefore be dissatisfied with their behavior, since their consumption of $640 billion assumed that their income would be only $800 billion and they would prefer to consume more out of the new, higher income. The increased consumption in turn increases income still further, with the process of expansion continuing until income reaches $900 billion.

The opposite process, contraction, would take place if consumers originally started with the expectation of an income of $1000 billion. They would spend $760 billion for consumption, yielding a total income to firms of $960 billion ($760 + $200 billion). When this income decrease was felt by consumers, they would decide that they had overspent their incomes and would contract spending to the lower level appropriate to the lower incomes. This contraction induces further contraction until incomes have fallen to $900 billion and consumption to $700 billion.

A great deal of confusion has revolved around the basic equations and whether they are always true or not. The answer is that Equation 4.1 is always true, for it merely expresses the definition of income as the sum of all expenditures. It therefore must be true, in exactly the same way that the population of New England *must* be the sum of the populations of the six states that are included in the equation cited in Chapter 1. The other equations, 4.2 and 4.3, indicate the intended behavior of consumers and investors, respectively. Since they represent behavior, they are true only if we allow sufficient time for the intended behavior to become actual behavior.

As an example, imagine that a small merchant checks his cash-register tape at noon and, on the basis of a half day's business, estimates his total income for the entire day. He calls his wife and tells her that she must do her shopping accordingly. She buys a number of things during the afternoon but passes up a hat she likes because she cannot afford it. That evening, the merchant adds his receipts and finds that his net income was $30 more than he had estimated. He and his wife now see that their actual expenditures were less than they would have been, had the estimate been correct. For this household, the consumption function does not hold today. But if we wait until morning, his wife will buy the hat. At that time, the actual behavior will match their intended behavior.

Other discrepancies might arise if shoppers are unable to buy the goods for which they are looking. Such difficulties might also face business and government purchasing agents.

Another difference between intended and actual behavior may result from unplanned change in inventories. In Chapter 2, we saw that businesses invest in inventories as well as in plant and equipment. Often such inventories may be part of a regular investment program. However, sometimes businesses buy (or make) goods for further sale and then are unable to find customers. In such cases, the businessman will find himself investing in inventories he does not want. In the other direction, a firm faced with a sudden rush of business may find that it has depleted its inventories (disinvested) to a greater extent than it wishes.

In all these cases, adjustments can be made if there is enough time. Usually, in fact, the time required for adjustment is quite short. Consumers can alter purchases and firms change their reorder patterns in a moderately short period of time. For this reason, we can ignore the discrepancies between actual and intended behavior if we are thinking of periods of, say, a year, but not if we look at shorter periods. These discrepancies are an important part of the pattern of adjustment toward the equilibrium level.

A complete understanding of our society would require that we direct especial attention to this adjustment process to determine whether it operates correctly and efficiently. Such study constitutes the heart of business-cycle research. Our present aim is to compare various equilibrium levels. We must leave to business-cycle analysis the precise study of how and whether the new equilibrium will be attained.

The Multiplier

One important application of the analysis given here is in examining changes in aggregate demand in comparison with changes in the unexplained variable, here investment. First, let us examine the effects of a change in investment. We start with the equation

$$Y = \frac{1}{1-b}(a + I_0) \tag{4.8}$$

We shall represent a change in investment by ΔI and the corresponding change in income by ΔY. Then, as investment increases from I_0 to

$I_0 + \Delta I$ income will increase from Y to $Y + \Delta Y$. Substituting these values in Equation 4.8 we obtain

$$Y + \Delta Y = \frac{1}{1 - b}(a + I_0 + \Delta I)$$

$$= \frac{1}{1 - b}(a + I_0) + \frac{1}{1 - b}\Delta I \qquad (4.9)$$

Subtracting Equation 4.8 from this, we obtain

$$\Delta Y = \frac{1}{1 - b}\Delta I \qquad (4.10)$$

This equation gives us the ratio between increases in investment and increases in income, which depends upon the marginal propensity to consume: b. On the basis of the figures presented in Tables 4.1 and 4.2, in which b equals $\frac{3}{5}$, this ratio will be $2\frac{1}{2}$. The reader can check this by referring to Table 4.2. If investment increases to 240, the equilibrium income will increase to 1000. In this case, the increase of 40 in investment causes an increase of 100 (or $2\frac{1}{2}$ times as much) in income.

This ratio between increases in income and investment is so important that economists have given it the name of the *multiplier*. We shall represent the multiplier by k. We can see from Equation 4.10 that

$$k = \frac{1}{1 - b} \qquad (4.11)$$

The multiplier gives the ratio of changes in equilibrium income to changes in investment. However, to remind ourselves that this is a summary of an economic process, not a juggling of simple algebra, it may be useful to trace the effects of an increase in investment upon income. We shall use a marginal propensity to consume, of $\frac{3}{5}$ and assume an initial investment of $100. This $100 becomes the income of some consumer who will spend $\frac{3}{5}$ of it, or $60. Similarly, the sum of $60 becomes income to another consumer who will spend $\frac{3}{5}$ of it, or $36. This process continues until the succeeding terms become too small to mention. Each of these can be treated as expenditure or as income. Eventually the total will expand by $250—the initial investment of $100 plus the successive increases in consumption, which total $150. The whole process follows the pattern described in Table 4.3.

TABLE 4.3

THE MULTIPLIER

Expenditure	Amount	Income
Initial Investment	$100.00	Income, consumer A
Consumption, consumer A	60.00	Income, consumer B
Consumption, consumer B	36.00	Income, consumer C
Consumption, consumer C	21.60	Income, consumer D
Consumption, consumer D	12.96	Income, consumer E
Consumption, consumer E	7.78	Income, consumer F
Consumption, consumer F	4.67	Income, consumer G
Total	$243.01	(or, eventually, $250.00)

Table 4.3 indicates that the income in each round serves as the basis of the consumption in the next. In this way, the entire process of expansion takes place as a multiple of the original spending. If consumers anticipate their higher incomes by increasing consumption before the new income is actually received, the entire process could take place almost simultaneously. If they follow rather conservative spending habits the expansionary process will take longer, but the result will be the same.

This example helps to illustrate two different uses of the multiplier concept. Table 4.3 illustrates the total effects of a single injection of spending, even though the effects are spread out in time. In our earlier discussions the multiplier was part of an equilibrium analysis, showing exactly what income would be consistent with a different level of investment. These two concepts are closely related, but they are not the same. Equilibrium income is that level where no forces tending to cause change are developed. If investment remained unchanged and the consumption function were unchanged, income would also remain unchanged. The multiplier of Table 4.3 tends to show what would happen in successive rounds if investment rose briefly and then fell back. However, if investment rose and stayed at the new level, the effects from previous periods would tend to accumulate. Such an accumulation is shown in Table 4.4.

In Table 4.4 it has been assumed that, in each period, the investment and consumption of the previous period have become someone's

TABLE 4.4

THE MULTIPLIER, CONTINUING INVESTMENT

Period	Invest-ment	Consumption, Based on Previous Period Investment	Consumption, Based on Previous Period Consumption	Total Consump-tion	Total Income
0	100.00	0.00	0.00	0.00	$100.00
1	100.00	60.00	0.00	60.00	$160.00
2	100.00	60.00	36.00	96.00	196.00
3	100.00	60.00	57.60	117.60	217.60
4	100.00	60.00	70.56	130.56	230.56
5	100.00	60.00	78.34	138.34	238.34
6	100.00	60.00	83.00	143.00	243.00
7	100.00	60.00	85.80	145.80	245.80
8	100.00	60.00	87.48	147.48	247.48
9	100.00	60.00	88.49	148.49	248.49
10	100.00	60.00	89.09	149.09	249.09
...	...	...	...	...	...
∞	100.00	60.00	90.00	150.00	250.00

income. This leads to additional consumption of an amount depending upon the marginal propensity to consume (still assumed to be 0.60). As long as income is below the final equilibrium level of $250.00 it will continue to grow, but when $250.00 is reached the growth would stop and the new level would be maintained indefinitely.

The Saving Function

Many economists prefer to speak of a saving function rather than of a consumption function. The choice between these terms involves largely a matter of taste rather than a difference in analysis. Since income is either saved or consumed, a decision about consumption is necessarily a decision about saving and vice versa. We can obtain the saving function from the consumption merely by subtracting consumption from income. Using S for saving,

$$\begin{aligned}
S &= Y - C \\
&= Y - (a + bY) \\
&= Y - a - bY \\
&= -a + (Y - bY) \\
&= -a + (1 - b)Y
\end{aligned} \tag{4.12}$$

The quantity $(1 - b)$ is the marginal propensity to save, the amount by which saving increases for every dollar of increased income. The first term, $-a$, gives the level of the saving function. The arithmetical computation of a saving function is presented in Table 4.5, using the consumption data of Table 4.1.

As indicated in Table 4.5, the saving column is obtained by subtracting the consumption at each income level from the income. Thus, for $700 billion, saving is $700 billion minus $580 billion, or $120 billion. The marginal propensity to save is the ratio of increased saving to the increased income for each interval. Since we have as-

TABLE 4.5

HYPOTHETICAL SAVING FUNCTION
(UNIT: $1 BILLION)

Income	Consumption	Saving	Marginal Propensity to Save
0	160	−160	
			0.40
100	220	−120	
			0.40
200	280	− 80	
			0.40
300	340	− 40	
			0.40
400	400	0	
			0.40
500	460	40	
			0.40
600	520	80	
			0.40
700	580	120	
			0.40
800	640	160	
			0.40
900	700	200	
			0.40
1000	760	240	

sumed straight lines, the marginal propensity to save is the same at all income levels. Notice that the marginal propensity to save, 0.40, is the complement of the marginal propensity to consume, 0.60; the sum of the two is always 1.00. This indicates that all income is either consumed or saved.

We can also obtain the saving function from the consumption function graphically. First draw a 45° line upward: the income line. The saving function is now obtained by subtracting the consumption function from the income line as illustrated in Figure 4.3. Note that when income exceeds consumption, saving is positive; when consumption is greater, saving is negative; and when consumption equals income, saving is zero. (Using the numbers of Table 4.5, this happens at an income of $400 billion.)

The multiplier can also be obtained from the saving relation. Using Equation 4.1 for the equilibrium conditions

$$Y = C + I_0 \tag{4.1}$$

we subtract C from both sides and obtain

$$Y - C = I_0$$
$$S = I_0 \tag{4.13}$$

Inserting the saving function of Equation 4.12,

$$-a + (1 - b)Y = I_0$$
$$(1 - b)Y = a + I_0 \tag{4.14}$$

This is the same as Equation 4.8. The rest of the process follows in the same fashion as in Equations 4.9 through 4.11.

A very simple solution technique using the saving function is shown in Table 4.6. Let us find the equilibrium income from the saving function of Table 4.5, again using the value of $200 billion for I_0. The equilibrium level is immediately seen to be $900 billion, for only at this level will saving match investment. Since investment is $200 billion, we need look only for the income level at which saving also equals $200 billion.

The corresponding graphic solution, demonstrated in Figure 4.4 is equally simple. If we draw a horizontal line to represent investment, the equilibrium income is found at the point at which the saving function crosses this line.

This solution technique corresponds to certain real forces in the economy. We saw in Chapter 2 that the saving-investment sector account always balances, that is, that *actual saving* always equals *actual investment*. We also noted that some of the saving and some

The Consumption Function and the Saving Function

FIGURE 4.3

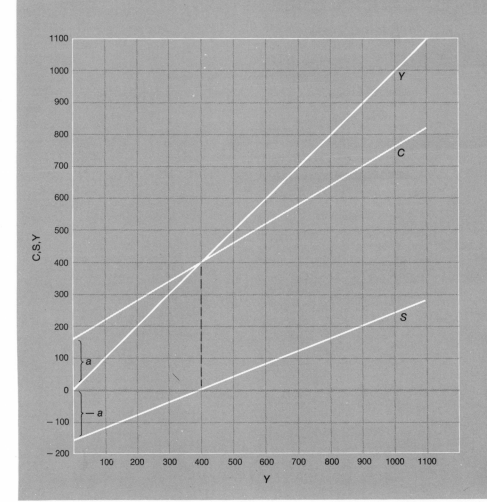

Equilibrium Income and Saving

FIGURE 4.4

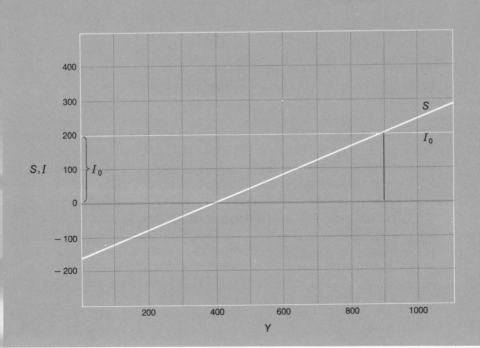

TABLE 4.6

HYPOTHETICAL INCOME DATA
(UNIT: $1 BILLION)

Y	S	I_0
0	−160	200
100	−120	200
200	− 80	200
300	− 40	200
400	0	200
500	40	200
600	80	200
700	120	200
800	160	200
900	200	200
1000	240	200

of the investment might be quite unintentional. Equilibrium can occur only when results match intentions. One can therefore identify equilibrium income as the point where *intended saving* equals *intended investment,* the point where the saving-investment sector account matches genuine plans.

cA Consumption Multiplier?

We have seen that it is possible to construct a multiplier that indicates the relation between changes in investment and changes in income. Can we then compute a multiplier that will give a relationship between the level of consumption and the level of income?

The answer to this question is both yes and no. The purpose of these multipliers is to show the reaction of the basic system to outside forces, the reaction of changes in the *endogenous* variables to changes in the *exogenous* variables. Consumption is not one of these outside forces but is rather a built-in feature of the system. To find the level of consumption, we need merely find the level of income, whereas the solution to the corresponding problem for investment requires a crystal ball, at least at this stage.

In a sense, it would be possible to compute something that is partly a consumption multiplier. Equation 4.2 told us that

$$C = a + bY \tag{4.2}$$

One might think of this equation as dividing consumption into two parts, one that does not depend upon income and one that does. (By analogy with the costs of a firm, we might call these *fixed consumption* and *variable consumption*.) The built-in part is the variable consumption; the fixed consumption might be regarded as exogenous. If so, one might use Equation 4.8—

$$Y = \frac{1}{1-b}(a + I_0) \tag{4.8}$$

to compute a multiplier

$$\Delta Y = \frac{1}{1-b}\Delta a \tag{4.15}$$

Such a multiplier would be the same as the investment multiplier. Since a is the constant that indicates the level of the consumption, this multiplier is of limited usefulness in indicating the reaction of national income to shifts in the level of the consumption function. Indeed, it is seldom applied; most economists find it simpler never to use the concept of a consumption multiplier.

Consumption and
The Classical System

The present analysis of the consumption function, although not inconsistent with the classical system, is irrelevant to it. If real income is determined by supply conditions, there is no point in considering what effect its change would have upon consumption. Only when our concept of aggregate supply is revised is it worthwhile to examine a consumption-income relationship. The classical discussion of consumption placed far more emphasis upon other factors, especially the interest rate, which will be discussed in Chapter 6.

Policy Implications

Even with such a simple model as the one given here it is possible to discuss a number of important policy questions. If, for example, the society is at a level that is $50 billion below full employment, the multiplier indicates the amount of investment stimulus which will be required to reach the full-employment level. Similarly, if demand exceeds available production, thus causing inflation, the multiplier indicates the magnitude of the task of reducing aggregate demand. In Chapter 5, we shall discuss the effects of those variables that are under government control.

PROBLEMS AND DISCUSSION QUESTIONS

1. If $C = 50 + \frac{3}{4}Y$, what is the saving function?
2. If $I = 200$ and $C = 50 + \frac{3}{4}Y$, what is the equilibrium income?
3. On the basis of the figures above, what is the multiplier?
4. Using Figure 4.2 as a model, draw a graph showing the equilibrium income for the examples above.
5. Using Figure 4.4 as a model, draw a graph showing equilibrium as demonstrated by the saving function.
6. Explain the reaction process in the economy if consumers suddenly decided to consume less (that is, if there is a decrease in a).

SUGGESTED ADDITIONAL READINGS

The simple Keynesian theory reviewed here can be found in most contemporary principles texts. It is derived from John Maynard Keynes, *The General Theory of Employment, Interest, and Money* (New York: Harcourt, 1936), Chapters 1, 3, and 10.

cAppendix to Chapter 4

BUSINESS SAVING

The time has now come to relax one of the assumptions with which we began this chapter, namely, that businesses pay out all incomes so that national product and personal income are equal. We observe that this is seldom the case. Depreciation is normally 7 to 9 percent of GNP. In addition, corporations often retain a substantial portion of their net earnings after tax for use in the business. These two, plus other forms of business saving, have accounted for nearly three-fourths of gross saving in recent years. One should therefore alter the system of three equations given at the beginning of this chapter in favor of the following set.

$$Y = C + I \tag{A4.1}$$
$$Y_D = Y - S_B \tag{A4.2}$$
$$S_P = -a_1 + (1 - b_1)Y_D \tag{A4.3}$$
$$S_B = -a_2 + (1 - b_2)Y \tag{A4.4}$$
$$Y_D = C + S_P \tag{A4.5}$$
$$I = I_0 \tag{A4.6}$$

NEW VARIABLES:

Y_D = Disposable Income
S_B = Business Saving
S_P = Personal Saving

59

Equations A4.1 and A4.2 are definitions. Equation A4.3 is the personal saving function given in the chapter, rewritten to relate saving to disposable income. Equation A4.4 is a business saving function, written in a form which corresponds to Equation A4.3. Equation A4.5 defines personal saving as the portion of disposable income not consumed. Equation A4.6 merely defines investment as exogenous.

In order to find the equilibrium condition, we can start with Equation A4.2 and insert the definitions of Y and Y_D from A4.1 and A4.5 respectively, then insert I_o from Equation A4.6.

$$Y_D = Y - S_B$$
$$C + S_P = C + I - S_B \tag{A4.7}$$
$$S_P + S_B = I_0$$

This equation is similar to Equation 4.13 except that saving is now split into two parts. Now insert the value of S_P from Equation A4.3

$$-a_1 + (1 - b_1)Y_D + S_B = I_0 \tag{A4.8}$$

Using the value of Y_D from Equation A4.2,

$$
\begin{aligned}
-a_1 + (1 - b_1)(Y - S_B) + S_B &= I_0 \\
-a_1 + (1 - b_1)Y - (1 - b_1)S_B + S_B &= I_0 \quad \text{(A4.9)} \\
-a_1 + (1 - b_1)Y + b_1 S_B &= I_0
\end{aligned}
$$

Now insert the value of S_B from Equation A4.4.

$$
\begin{aligned}
-a_1 + (1 - b_1)Y + b_1[-a_2 + (1 - b_2)Y] &= I_0 \\
-a_1 + (1 - b_1)Y - a_2 b_1 + b_1(1 - b_2)Y &= I_0 \\
-a_1 - a_2 b_1 + (1 - b_1 + b_1 - b_1 b_2)Y &= I_0 \\
-(a_1 + a_2 b_1) + (1 - b_1 b_2)Y &= I_0
\end{aligned}
$$
$$\tag{A4.10}$$

Equation A4.10 is similar in form to Equation 4.14. Saving is a linear function of income and is equal to investment. The difference is that now the coefficients of the saving function depend upon the behavior of business savers and individual savers.

In future chapters, the saving function will be given in the form used earlier in the chapter. We must remember, however, that a and b are composite coefficients, combining business and household saving into one measure.

5

Fiscal Policy

This chapter is concerned with the role of the government in determining the over-all level of aggregate demand. In the last chapter we assumed a very simplified economy without government. We now wish to add in the role of the government budget. Governments, with their expenditures, taxes, and transfer payments, are a very important sector of the economy, and we wish to consider their effects. In addition, in the last thirty years, governments have increasingly used this budget as a tool to control the economy. However, the government sector remains exogenous to an economist. We can only examine its effects on the rest of the economy. We shall use the following system:

ADDITIONAL VARIABLES:

Endogenous:

Y_D = Disposable Income

Exogenous:

G = Government Expenditures

Tx = Taxes

Tr = Transfers

EQUATIONS

$$Y = C + I + G \tag{5.1}$$
$$C = a + bY_D \tag{5.2}$$
$$Y_D = Y - Tx + Tr \tag{5.3}$$
$$I = I_0 \tag{5.4}$$
$$G = G_0 \tag{5.5}$$
$$Tx = Tx_0 \tag{5.6}$$
$$Tr = Tr_0 \tag{5.7}$$

As the statistics presented in Chapter 2 demonstrate, the various levels of government—local, state, and federal—have played an increasingly important role in the American economy. In recent years, governments have purchased 20 to 25 percent of all goods and services produced in our country. More than half this total has been purchased by the federal government and the remainder by state and local governments. Since such an enormous portion of national purchasing power is concentrated under relatively centralized control, the many suggestions that this power be used to affect the level of demand are not surprising. The manipulation of government income and expenditures for the maintenance of a suitable level of income is called *fiscal policy*.

There are, of course, many other ways in which the government can affect national income. Every government activity is apt to have some effect upon the level of national income. An antitrust case that breaks up a monopoly may lead to lower prices and increased output. A new trade treaty could affect the output of our import and export industries and of those industries whose products compete with the imported goods. We confine ourselves to the field of fiscal policy, therefore, merely for the sake of convenience and not because other activities are unimportant. In the long run the general tenor of the society, as indicated by the other activities of the government, may be far more important than fiscal policy.

Even within this narrow range of fiscal policy we shall confine ourselves to some rather simple assumptions. We shall initially speak of changes in taxes without discussing the various kinds of taxes, even though the differences among them are important. For our purposes a tax is any device for transferring money from the pockets of consumers to the coffers of the government without any direct return to the consumer. (This last qualification is intended to eliminate from the list of taxes, government income received from the post office and other such agencies. Remember, however, that the national accounts treat the profits of these enterprises as taxes, since the entire profits go to the government.)

The government budget then consists of three main items: government expenditures, transfers, and taxes. Government expenditures are limited to payments for goods and services. They include such items as salaries of government officials, payments for transportation, and the purchase of millions of items from jet bombers to paper clips. Transfer payments are those payments that are made without any receipt of goods or services by the government, at least in the year in which the payment is made. Transfers include welfare payments; unemployment compensation; pensions to old soldiers; and, with doubtful validity, interest on the government debt. Taxes, as indicated above, are payments to the government for which the taxpayer receives no direct return. Taxes are therefore exactly the reverse of transfers. The distinguishing element of each is a flow of money unmatched by a corresponding flow of goods. In some cases, we can even match types of transfers with types of taxes to show the similarity of the two elements. A business subsidy (transfer) is just the opposite of a business tax; unemployment compensation is a negative income tax. Thus we should expect, and shall find, that transfers have exactly the same effects as taxes, but in the opposite direction.

There is a great temptation among students to insist on relating the sum totals of government receipts and of government expenditures to each other. However, it is not always true that such a relation exists. So long as a government has the power to borrow there is no reason to assume that its receipts and expenditures will exactly match in any one year. New expenditures may be financed by borrowing, as are many turnpike projects, new taxes may be used to reduce debt; governments may borrow to finance relief payments. Indeed, the federal government, which has the power to create money, could operate an unbalanced budget forever, printing new money to cover the deficit. (The advisability of such a course is debatable and will be discussed later. It is, however, constitutionally possible.)

Since governments have demonstrated their ability to vary one portion of the budget without a corresponding change in other portions, we shall consider changes in government expenditures, transfers, and taxes separately. Thus, when we say that an increase in government expenditures has a certain effect, this is true *other things being equal*. In particular, we assume no change in taxes. For example, we say that increased taxes are deflationary (that is, they tend to lower national income), but if these higher taxes cause increased government expenditures, the effect of the whole program may be mildly expansionary.

Government Expenditures

In Chapter 4 we found an investment multiplier. Because government expenditures appear in the equations in exactly the same way as investment, we should therefore expect that the government expenditures multiplier would be the same as the investment multiplier:

$$k_G = \frac{1}{1-b} \tag{5.8}$$

(In Chapter 4 we designated this multiplier as k. In this chapter we shall be discussing many different multipliers and therefore have designated this one k_G to indicate that it is the multiplier for government expenditures.) This multiplier indicates the change in aggregate demand per dollar of change in government expenditures. The sign of the multiplier is positive, indicating that an increase in government expenditures will increase income and that, conversely, a decrease in government expenditure will decrease income.

Taxes and Transfers

Before examining the tax and transfer multipliers, let us consider the problem intuitively. A government transfer puts money into the hands of consumers exactly as would a government expenditure of the same magnitude. The consumers in both cases respend a portion of the money, thereby increasing the incomes of others and increasing their expenditures. Thus, the effects on consumption are the same whether the government hires an accountant or pays a pension to a retired general. The difference between the two cases is that government expenditures bring about increased production of goods and services, whereas the transfers do not. (In the example above, the accountant must work for his money; the general need not.) If a government expenditure of $100 brings about a $250 increase in income, we would expect it to consist of an increase of $100 in government goods or services and $150 in consumer goods. A transfer payment of $100 causes the same $150 increase in consumption but no increase in government goods and services. In this case, the government-expenditures multiplier is $2\frac{1}{2}$ and the transfer multiplier is $1\frac{1}{2}$.

Regardless of the size of the consumption effect, it is clear that the difference between the expenditure multiplier and the transfer multiplier results from the inclusion of the original $100 in the pattern for government expenditures, but not in that resulting from the transfer payment. Therefore, the transfer multiplier will always be exactly 1 less than the government-expenditures multiplier. The complete derivation of the transfer multiplier is contained in the Appendix. However, it follows from the discussion above that

$$
\begin{aligned}
k_{Tr} &= k_G - 1 \\
&= \frac{1}{1-b} - 1 = \frac{1}{1-b} - \frac{1-b}{1-b} \\
&= \frac{b}{1-b}
\end{aligned}
\tag{5.9}
$$

The tax multiplier is numerically the same as the transfer multiplier but its opposite in sign. The transfer multiplier is positive, indicating that an increase in transfers will increase national income. We have already noted that taxes are the opposite of transfers: taxes shift money from consumers to the government whereas transfers shift it from the government to consumers. This symmetry indicates that the tax multiplier is the same as the transfer multiplier but negative. The negative multiplier means that an increase in taxes will decrease income and vice versa. Again, formal derivation is relegated to the Appendix, but it is clear that

$$
k_{Tx} = -\frac{b}{1-b}
\tag{5.10}
$$

Equilibrium Income

From the equations at the beginning of this chapter it is clear that the principal change from Chapter 4 is in the consumption function. Instead of relating consumption directly to income, we have substituted a function in which consumption is related to *disposable income*, or take-home pay. This substitution is a step in the direction of greater realism, especially since income and social security taxes are withheld. It suggests that individuals plan their consumption by examining money they actually receive—earned income after taxes plus pensions and other such unearned income.

We can use the preceding discussion and the equations of this chapter to summarize the impact of government fiscal variables. Government expenditures add to the total spending flow in exactly the same way as investment. Therefore changes in government purchases affect national income the same as investment, that is, by an amount equal to the increase times the multiplier. Taxes are a deduction from income before obtaining disposable income. Consumption depends upon this lower amount. Therefore the effect of taxes is to lower national income, but by a smaller multiplier.

An illustration of these changes is given in Tables 5.1 and 5.2. In Table 5.1, we have assumed that taxes and transfers are equal so that net taxes are zero. (Do not worry about the realism of this example; it has been chosen only for purposes of illustration.) The consumption function is the same one used in Chapter 4. Investment (I_0) is assumed to be $90 billion and government purchases (G_0) $110 billion. Equilibrium will come when income equals the sum of consumption, investment, and government spending. In this case, equi-

TABLE 5.1

HYPOTHETICAL INCOME DATA
(UNIT: $1 BILLION)

$Y = Y_D$	C	I_0	G_0	$C + I_0 + G_0$
0	160	90	110	360
100	220	90	110	420
200	280	90	110	480
300	340	90	110	540
400	400	90	110	600
500	460	90	110	660
600	520	90	110	720
700	580	90	110	780
800	640	90	110	840
900	700	90	110	900
1000	760	90	110	960

librium is at $900 billion. If G_0 were to increase to 150, equilibrium income would increase to 1000, demonstrating a multiplier of $2\frac{1}{2}$ (an increase of 100 in income divided by the increase of 40 in government purchases).

The effects of taxes (and transfers) are illustrated in Table 5.2. The same numbers as in Table 5.1 are used with lower values omitted and intermediate values inserted, except that net taxes (taxes minus transfers) are assumed to be $100 billion. For each level of income, one finds disposable income by subtracting $100 billion of net taxes. The appropriate consumption is found and added to investment and government purchases. The equilibrium income is that at which $Y = C + I_0 + G_0$, in this example $750 billion. By comparing Table 5.2 with Table 5.1, we see that the *increase* in taxes of $100 billion led to a *decrease* in income of $150 billion, indicating a tax multiplier of minus $1\frac{1}{2}$.

No separate illustration will be given for transfers. It should be clear than an increase in transfers of, say, 40 would decrease the net tax by 40 and raise disposable income by the same amount. This would lead to an increase in consumption of 24. Further rounds of consumption increase would bring an ultimate increase of 60.

The graphic solution to this problem is substantially similar to the numerical examples of Tables 5.1 and 5.2. The white lines of

TABLE 5.2

HYPOTHETICAL INCOME AND TAX DATA
(UNIT: $1 BILLION)

Y	$Tx - Tr$	Y_D	C	I_0	G_0	$C + I_0 + G_0$
500	100	400	400	90	110	600
550	100	450	430	90	110	630
600	100	500	460	90	110	660
650	100	550	490	90	110	690
700	100	600	520	90	110	720
750	100	650	550	90	110	750
800	100	700	580	90	110	780
850	100	750	610	90	110	810
900	100	800	640	90	110	840
950	100	850	670	90	110	870
1000	100	900	700	90	110	900

Figure 5.1 correspond to Table 5.1; the heavy lines, to Table 5.2. In each case, I_0 and G_0 are added to the consumption line and the equilibrium is found where $C + I_0 + G_0$ crosses the 45° line. (Notice the similarity to Figure 4.2.)

The heavy lines represent the effects of an increase in taxes of $100 billion. This effect is recorded by moving the consumption line *horizontally* by the amount of the tax. In the present case, an income of $600 billion represents a disposable income of $500 billion (see Table 5.2) and a consumption of $460 billion. Thus a consumption of 460 is plotted against an income of 600, rather than against 500 as in the white line.

Taxes and Saving

The effects of either taxes or transfers on saving are very similar to their effects on consumption. First, let us redefine saving:

$$S = Y_D - C$$
$$= Y - Tx + Tr - C \tag{5.11}$$

This is in keeping with the previous discussion in this chapter, which implied that consumption depends upon disposable income, not upon earned income. This will, however, change the equilibrium condition slightly. This condition requires that

$$Y = C + I + G \tag{5.12}$$

Solving Equation 5.11 for Y, one finds that

$$Y = C + S + Tx - Tr \tag{5.13}$$

Substituting this value into Equation 5.12

$$C + S + Tx - Tr = C + I + G \tag{5.14}$$

or

$$S + Tx - Tr = I + G \tag{5.15}$$

The Effect of Taxes on Equilibrium Income

FIGURE 5.1

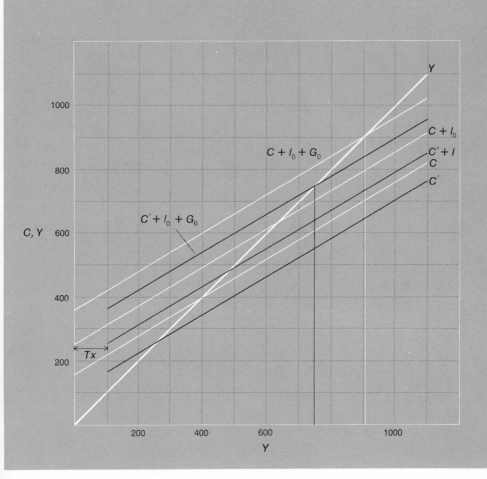

This, then, is the new equilibrium condition. In appearance it seems rather unlike the equilibrium equation presented in Chapter 4. In meaning, however, it is similar. Equation 5.15 shows that net outside sources of expenditures $I + G$ must equal the net withdrawals of consumers S plus the net withdrawals of the government $Tx - Tr$ from the income stream. It is convenient to refer to investment and government spending as *injections* into the spending stream; they do not depend on the circular flow in the way consumption does. On the other side, saving and net taxes represent *leakages* from the circular flow. The equilibrium occurs when the planned leakages equal the planned injections.

Tables 5.3 and 5.4 show the method of finding equilibrium income by the use of saving, using the data of Tables 5.1 and 5.2 respectively. In each case, the injections—investment and government spending— are added together. Then these must be compared with the leakages. In Table 5.3, saving is the only leakage. The equilibrium income is \$900 billion where saving of \$200 billion just matches the \$200 billion injections. In Table 5.4, the net tax of \$100 billion is subtracted from the income to obtain disposable income. The saving appropriate to each level of disposable income is found and then added to the

TABLE 5.3

HYPOTHETICAL INCOME AND SAVING DATA
(UNIT: \$1 BILLION)

$Y = Y_D$	S	I_0	G_0	$I_0 + G_0$
0	-160	90	110	200
100	-120	90	110	200
200	-80	90	110	200
300	-40	90	110	200
400	0	90	110	200
500	40	90	110	200
600	80	90	110	200
700	120	90	110	200
800	160	90	110	200
900	200	90	110	200
1000	240	90	110	200

TABLE 5.4

HYPOTHETICAL INCOME, SAVING AND TAX DATA
(UNIT: $1 BILLION)

Y	$Tx - Tr$	Y_D	S	$S + (Tx - Tr)$	$I_0 + G_0$
500	100	400	0	100	200
550	100	450	20	120	200
600	100	500	40	140	200
650	100	550	60	160	200
700	100	600	80	180	200
750	100	650	100	200	200
800	100	700	120	220	200
850	100	750	140	240	200
900	100	800	160	260	200
950	100	850	180	280	200
1000	100	900	200	300	200

net tax to find the total leakage. The equilibrium income is that at which the total leakage equals the total injections, in this case at $750 billion. Comparing Tables 5.3 and 5.4, we see that the income has decreased by $150 billion as a result of the $100 billion tax, for a multiplier of $1\frac{1}{2}$, corresponding to a marginal propensity to consume of 0.6.

The same solution is presented in Figure 5.2. The horizontal white lines represent the injections—investment and government spending. The sloping white line, marked S, represents the saving schedule of Table 5.3, with no tax. The equilibrium income is $900 billion. The heavy line, S', represents the lower saving resulting from taxes. This line represents S moved to the right by 100, since the same level of saving takes place only at an income 100 higher than before. The second heavy line, $S' + Tx$, indicates the addition of taxes to this new level of saving, to find the total leakage. The new equilibrium, $750 billion, occurs where the new total leakage equals the total injections.

By looking at Figure 5.2, we find that at every income level the new saving plus the tax is higher than the old saving, so that leakages increase. This is what we should expect, since a part of the tax falls

Taxes and Saving

FIGURE 5.2

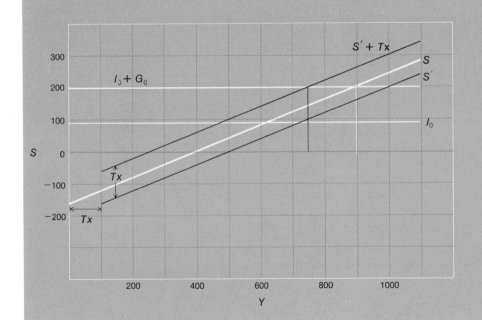

on consumption. Using a marginal propensity to consume of 0.6, a tax of $100 billion would reduce consumption by $60 billion and saving by $40 billion. The total leakages would therefore increase by $60 billion, the increase in tax minus the decrease in saving. Thus the new equilibrium is less than the equilibrium before the tax increase.

cAutomatic Stabilizers

A government budget in which taxes; transfers; and, sometimes, government expenditures change with national income is said to contain automatic stabilizers. The object of such a system is to lessen the impact of changes in investment upon the national income. The actual calculation of an adjusted multiplier will be postponed to the Appendix, but let us consider the impact of such a system here.

In a system with these automatic stabilizers, all reactions would be expected to be more sluggish than otherwise. If the marginal rate of taxation were 25 percent, a decline in earned income of $100 would result in a decline in disposable income of only $75. The resulting change in consumption would be $45, compared with the $60 that it would have been in the absence of changes in taxes. The multiplier will also be less, since it is based on the effective change in consumption of only 45 percent of the change in income. Such a multiplier would have a value of only 1.82 instead of 2.50.

Table 5.5 gives a comparison of multiplier values with and without variable taxation. The *effective* marginal propensity to consume is arrived at by multiplying the marginal propensity to consume by the marginal rate of retention, that is, by 1 minus the tax rate. The difference in the multiplier for zero tax rates and the other values indicates the effect of the built-in adjustment.

Figure 5.3 demonstrates the impact of automatic stabilizers on the economy. As income rises, taxes rise also. This has the effect of making the $S' + Tx$ line (the total leakage line) steeper. The increased steepness means that a given change in injections will cause less shift in income.

These automatic stabilizers have become an important tool of modern fiscal policy. If the government financial program is designed so that taxes fall and transfers rise with every decline in national

TABLE 5.5

AUTOMATIC STABILIZERS

Marginal Propensity to Consume	Marginal Rate of Taxation	Effective Marginal Propensity to Consume	Multiplier
0.8	0.0	0.80	5.00
0 8	0.1	0.72	3.57
0.8	0.2	0.64	2.78
0.8	0.3	0.56	2.28
0.6	0.0	0.60	2.50
0.6	0.1	0.54	2.18
0.6	0.2	0.48	1.92
0.6	0.3	0.42	1.72
0.4	0.0	0.40	1.67
0.4	0.1	0.36	1.56
0.4	0.2	0.32	1.47
0.4	0.3	0.28	1.39

income, the induced changes in income will be smaller. Such a program helps to keep recessions from becoming depressions. Excise, income, and payroll taxes have this feature, as does unemployment insurance. Property and poll taxes do not have it, neither do transfer payments such as pensions, based purely on age or service.

The attractive part of such a program is the built-in feature. Although the multiplier is lessened, it remains greater than 1 unless the marginal propensity to consume is zero or the marginal rate of taxation is 100 percent. Therefore, it is not possible by such a program to eliminate all fluctuations in income. On the other hand, it is possible to eliminate these fluctuations by a suitable program of change in tax *rates* or government spending. However, these changes require executive planning and, usually, legislative approval, both of which take time and necessitate correct forecasting techniques. The built-in features, on the other hand, operate automatically, immediately, and without the necessity of prediction.

Automatic Stabilizers

FIGURE 5.3

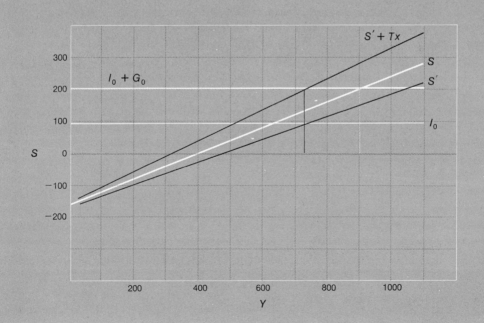

Balanced Budget

In public discussions about government activity, we sometimes hear the statement that inflation or depression could be avoided if every change in government spending were matched by a corresponding change in taxes. Our previous discussions should convince us that this is not the case, since the multipliers for government expenditures and for taxes are not the same. If the government were to embark upon a program of spending when, and only when, it had tax revenue to cover the spending, then we could say that the government had a marginal propensity to consume of 1. Since the marginal propensity of the average taxpayer is less than this, the flow of spending will increase. Thus, increased spending is inflationary even if it is matched by increased taxes. The exact amount of the expansionary effect can be obtained from the multipliers. Let government expenditures and taxes both increase by an amount X, that is,

$$\Delta G = \Delta Tx = X \tag{5.16}$$

Then the increase in income will be the sum of the effects of the increase in both—that is

$$\Delta Y = k_G X + k_{Tx} X \tag{5.17}$$

letting k_G and k_{Tx} represent the expenditures multiplier and the tax multiplier respectively. Using the values obtained in Equations 5.8 and 5.10,

$$\begin{aligned}
\Delta Y &= \frac{1}{1-b} X - \frac{b}{1-b} X \\
&= \frac{1-b}{1-b} X \\
&= X
\end{aligned} \tag{5.18}$$

From the foregoing, we can see that the balanced-budget multiplier is exactly 1, regardless of the marginal propensity to consume. This follows logically from the fact that the tax multiplier is always one less than the government-expenditure multiplier. If the government takes away money and then respends it for goods and services, the money in the hands of consumers is unchanged and so is the entire sequence of later consumer spending. However, total product will be increased by the goods and services the government received back for its spending.

A Final Caution

The preceding discussion has centered around the effects of changes in government fiscal variables assuming that other factors do not change. As we shall see in Chapter 7, it is very unlikely that investment would be unaffected by changes in government fiscal variables. In the interests of simplicity, however, in our discussion of the effect of the fiscal changes we shall assume that investment is unchanged. After the groundwork has been prepared we shall then consider the effects of any resultant change in investment as an added factor (see Chapter 15).

Within this limited framework our conclusions are limited still more, to the mechanics of government fiscal policy. The only conclusions to be drawn deal with what the government *can* do, not with what it *should* do. The government *can* provide any desired level of aggregate demand; many citizens argue that it *should* not do so, because, they claim, such actions are a step down the road to socialism; or because it would be better to encourage private initiative; or because government may misdirect spending into the wrong channels. But we cannot discuss here the complete role of government in the economy. Some of its aspects require additional analysis, and we shall discuss them in more detail later. Many of them depend upon value judgments, and the most that an economist can do is to point out what the alternatives are.

This distinction between *can* and *should* is the source of most of the confusion over the term *Keynesian*. To the extent that he follows the preceding analysis of what *can* be done, virtually every economist is a Keynesian. To the extent that they believe the government *should* affect national income in one or more ways, at one particular time or always, different economists are Keynesian to different degrees. In the sense of advocating high government expenditures at all times, it is doubtful if there has ever been a Keynesian, even Lord Keynes. Economists are in substantial agreement in the analytical areas. In policy recommendations, they agree on what ought to be done about as often and as rarely as other citizens.

PROBLEMS AND DISCUSSION QUESTIONS

In the first five problems below, assume that $C = 50 + \frac{3}{4}Y_D$, $I = 120$, and $G = 40$.

1. If taxes are 20 and transfers zero, what is the equilibrium level of income?

2. Draw two graphs finding this equilibrium, using Figures 5.1 and 5.2 as models.

3. If the government wishes to push income to 1100, by how much must it alter government spending? Transfer payments? Taxes?

4. If the government increases spending by $40 billion and finances half the increase by taxation, how much will income change?

5. If taxes equal $-20 + 0.10Y$, what is the investment multiplier? What is equilibrum income?

6. What kinds of transfer payments are part of our system of automatic stabilizers? Which are not?

7. Is the automatic stabilizing character of our tax system altered by changes in family exemptions for income taxes? By changes in income-tax rates?

8. What nonincome taxes contribute to automatic stabilization?

SUGGESTED ADDITIONAL READINGS

The balanced-budget multiplier was first pointed out in Trygve Haavelmo, "Multiplier Effects of a Balanced Budget," *Econometrica*, vol. 13 (1945). *See also* the subsequent discussion in the April 1946 issue of the same journal.

Among the leading advocates of automatic stabilizers is the Committee for Economic Development, a business group concerned with economic and fiscal policy. For comments on its proposals *see* O. H. Brownlee, "The C. E. D. on Federal Tax Reform," *Journal of Political Economy*, vol. 56 (1948), and Walter W. Heller, "The C. E. D.'s Stabilizing Budget Policy after 10 Years," *American Economic Review*, 47 (1957), pp. 634–651.

On the general problems of fiscal policy *see* the annual *Economic Report of the President* and the subsequent hearings by the Joint Economic Committee of the Congress.

$c\mathcal{A}$ppendix to Chapter 5

DERIVATION OF MULTIPLIERS

To compute the multipliers for each of the three government variables—expenditures, transfers, and taxes—we start with the system of equations given at the beginning of Chapter 5:

$$Y = C + I + G \tag{5.1}$$
$$C = a + bY_D \tag{5.2}$$
$$Y_D = Y - Tx + Tr \tag{5.3}$$
$$I = I_0 \tag{5.4}$$
$$G = G_0 \tag{5.5}$$
$$Tx = Tx_0 \tag{5.6}$$
$$Tr = Tr_0 \tag{5.7}$$

First, we substitute Equations 5.6 and 5.7 into Equation 5.3, and Equation 5.3 into Equation 5.2:

$$
\begin{aligned}
C &= a + bY_D \\
&= a + b(Y - Tx_0 + Tr_0) \\
&= a + bY - bTx_0 + bTr_0
\end{aligned} \tag{A5.1}
$$

Now we substitute Equations A5.1, 5.4, and 5.5 into Equation 5.1:

$$
\begin{aligned}
Y &= C + I + G \\
&= a + bY - bTx_0 + bTr_0 + I_0 + Go
\end{aligned} \tag{A5.2}
$$

Simplifying Equation A5.2

$$Y - bY = a - bTx_0 + bTr_0 + I_0 + G_0 \qquad \text{(A5.3)}$$
$$(1 - b)Y = a - bTx_0 + bTr_0 + I_0 + G_0 \qquad \text{(A5.4)}$$
$$Y = \frac{1}{1 - b}(a - bTx_0 + bTr_0 + I_0 + G_0) \quad \text{(A5.5)}$$

To obtain the government-expenditures multiplier, increase G_0 to $G_0 + \Delta G$, and Y will increase to $Y + \Delta Y$.

$$
\begin{aligned}
Y + \Delta Y &= \frac{1}{1 - b} \\
&\quad (a - bTx_0 + bTr_0 + I_0 + G_0 + \Delta G) \\
&= \frac{1}{1 - b}(a - bTx_0 + bTr_0 + I_0 + G_0) \\
&\quad\quad\quad\quad + \frac{1}{1 - b}\Delta G \quad \text{(A5.6)}
\end{aligned}
$$

Subtracting Equation A5.5 from Equation A5.6,

$$\Delta Y = \frac{1}{1 - b}\Delta G \qquad\qquad\qquad \text{(A5.7)}$$

To obtain the transfer multiplier, increase Tr_0 to $Tr_0 + \Delta Tr$, with the corresponding shift in Y

$$
\begin{aligned}
Y + \Delta Y &= \frac{1}{1 - b} \\
&\quad (a - bTx_0 + bTr_0 + b\Delta Tr + I_0 + G_0) \\
&= \frac{1}{1 - b}(a - bTx_0 + bTr_0 + I_0 + G_0) \\
&\quad\quad\quad\quad + \frac{1}{1 - b}(b\Delta Tr) \quad \text{(A5.8)}
\end{aligned}
$$

Subtracting Equation A5.5

$$\Delta Y = \frac{1}{1 - b}(b\Delta Tr) = \frac{b}{1 - b}\Delta Tr \qquad\qquad \text{(A5.9)}$$

In the same way, we compute the tax relation

$$\Delta Y = -\frac{b}{1 - b}\Delta Tx \qquad\qquad\qquad\qquad \text{(A5.10)}$$

From Equations A5.7, A5.9, and A5.10, we find the appropriate multipliers

$$\textbf{Expenditures:} \quad k_G = \frac{1}{1-b} \tag{A5.11}$$

$$\textbf{Transfers:} \quad k_{Tr} = \frac{b}{1-b} \tag{A5.12}$$

$$\textbf{Taxes:} \quad k_{Tx} = -\frac{b}{1-b} \tag{A5.13}$$

In order to recalculate the multiplier with automatic stabilizers, we assume, for simplicity, no transfers. The system then consists of

$$Y = C + I + G \tag{5.1}$$
$$C = a + bY_D \tag{5.2}$$
$$Y_D = Y - Tx + Tr \tag{5.3}$$
$$I = I_0 \tag{5.4}$$
$$G = G_0 \tag{5.5}$$
$$Tx = T_0 + hY \tag{A5.14}$$
$$Tr = 0 \tag{A5.15}$$

Note that h represents the marginal rate of taxation. Substituting Equations A5.14 and A5.15 into Equation 5.3, and 5.3 into 5.2:

$$\begin{aligned} C &= a + b(Y - T_0 - hY) \\ &= a + bY - bT_0 - bhY \\ &= a - bT_0 + bY - bhY \end{aligned} \tag{A5.16}$$

Substituting Equations 5.4, 5.5, and A5.16 into Equation 5.1:

$$Y = a - bT_0 + bY - bhY + I_0 + G_0 \tag{A5.17}$$
$$Y - bY + bhY = a - bT_0 + I_0 + G_0 \tag{A5.18}$$
$$Y = \frac{1}{1 - b + bh}(a - bT_0 + I_0 + G_0) \tag{A5.19}$$

Thus, the investment multiplier with automatic stabilizers is

$$k_I = \frac{1}{1 - b + bh} = \frac{1}{(1-b)(1-h) + h} \tag{A5.20}$$

Since h is the marginal rate of taxation, $(1 - h)$ represents the marginal rate of retention, the percentage of additional income which is kept. Since $(1 - b)$ is the marginal propensity to save disposable income, $(1 - b)(1 - h)$ is the effective marginal propensity to save earned income. We therefore see that the denominator of the multiplier is equal to the sum of the effective marginal propensity to save and the marginal tax rate, the two leakage ratios.

6

Consumption

Our principal concern in this book is to study the interrelationships of various aggregate variables. For this purpose, the simplified consumption function of Chapter 5, showing consumption as a linear function of income, is adequate. But macroeconomics also deals with attempts to find comparatively exact measures of these functions and to forecast their levels. It is therefore important to consider the impact of other variables upon consumption, even though all of these other variables may be treated as exogenous. The increasing use of econometric forecasting models requires such an extended range of study.

Types of Consumption

In the national income statistics of the Department of Commerce, consumption goods are classified in two different ways. The first classification groups these goods according to the type of expenditure they represent, such as food, clothing, and the like. For some detailed analyses, this grouping is very useful. In attempting an over-all survey, it is usually more profitable to classify goods according to the type of product—that is, durable goods, nondurable goods, and services. Figure 6.1 illustrates the changes in consumption over the years.

These product divisions are not completely precise. Ordinarily, one would say that a television set is a durable good and that television repair is a service. But if the set is sold with a one-year guarantee, the entire cost is usually subsumed under the classification of a durable good, although it is clear that a portion of the payment reimburses the seller for the expected cost of repairs. We should therefore regard this method of classification as an approximate one. None of the discussion in this chapter will assume any great precision in this type of grouping.

For purposes of economic analysis, the most important distinction is between durable goods on the one hand and nondurable goods and services on the other. For the latter group, the purchase and the actual use of the goods is almost simultaneous. The time elapsed between purchasing a ticket and seeing a play or motion picture may be only a matter of minutes and is seldom more than a few days. Similarly, most foods are purchased for use within a week or two at most.

Durable goods are of a different type, for they are used for many years after their purchase. This range of time between purchase and use causes many problems. In Chapter 2 we discussed the problem it raises for statisticians: should consumption be measured at the time of purchase or at use? The statisticians agreed to base their measurements on the time of purchase, since that is the time at which income is produced for the seller. It is also, in any case, the easiest time to measure. (Only for houses does the treatment differ. Since there is a well-developed rental market for houses, all purchases of houses are treated as investment and their rental value is treated as consumption. For owner-occupied houses, this means imputing a fictitious rental payment by the owner to himself.)

For the analysis of national income, the statisticians' decision is the correct one. The influence of a purchase on the economy comes at the time of purchase. Even if the buyer keeps his new refrigerator in the crate, businesses have made profits, workers have been hired, and materials have been used. However, we cannot ignore these goods once they have been sold. One of the important factors in determining sales of such goods is the stock already in the hands of consumers. We will therefore give especial attention to these goods.

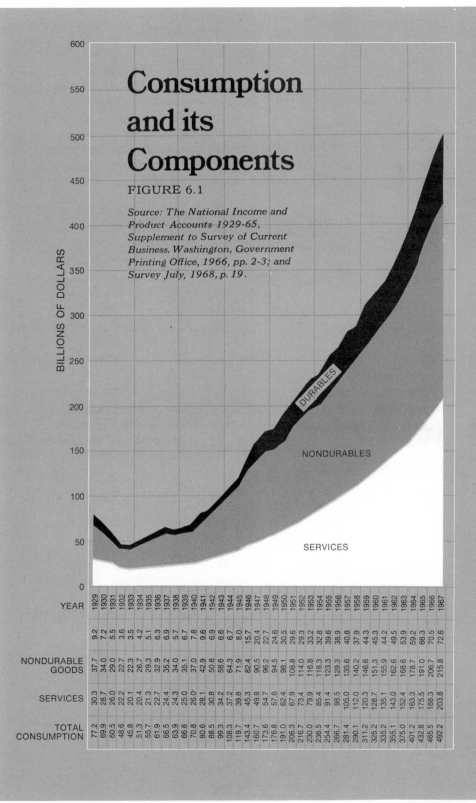

Durable Assets

In general, one may say that the existence of a large stock of durable goods in the hands of consumers tends to lessen consumption expenditures. The more durable goods one owns, the fewer he wishes to purchase. We should therefore expect to find that two families with exactly the same income but with different stocks of durables would spend differently. Similarly, we should expect the national consumption function to be higher after a depression or a war when people have depleted their stocks of durables, than after a boom when families are generally well stocked.

One suggested method of explaining purchases of goods is to assume that the stock of durables that people would like to have is related to their income. The actual purchases would then be some portion of the difference between this desired stock and the stock that they already own. This method was used many years ago to predict automobile sales. Unfortunately, it does not lend itself well to statistical study because of the difficulty of measuring what people would like. A simpler method is to assume that the *purchases* are related to income but that the *level* of purchases is related to the stock of durable goods. (In the usual consumption function, $C = a + bY$, this means that the stock of durable goods affects the size of a; the larger the stock, the smaller is a.)

Thus far we have been considering the effects of the stock of durable goods on the purchases of more durables. The stock of durables also affects consumption of nondurable goods and services.

The possession of most durable goods tends to lessen the need for other consumption. A family with home-laundry equipment has less demand for commercial-laundry services. The total expenditure for food of a family with a home freezer may possibly be decreased. One of the most interesting shifts of this type in recent years has been the substitution of television for commercial entertainment, especially motion pictures. Over a somewhat longer period, private automobiles have substituted for commercial transportation, especially rail travel.

In some respects, however, the possession of certain durable goods may increase consumption of other products that are used jointly with the durable good. This joint-cost element is most important in the case of automobiles, for fuel and maintenance costs usually exceed the cost of the vehicle itself. The increased use of electrically operated durables is an important element in the increased home consumption of electricity. It is probable that, on balance, automobiles increase other consumption whereas other durables decrease consumption.

cMonetary Assets

Monetary assets are not normally considered consumer goods. (We will ignore the pleasure the miser receives from contemplating his hoard.) Instead, these assets affect behavior primarily because they affect the wealth of the consumer and therefore alter his willingness to spend. In this category we include cash; bank deposits; government and private bonds; personal notes and mortgages; stocks; and, to some extent, jewels and works of art.

In general, one would say that possession of larger monetary assets would increase the willingness of consumers to consume current income. There is no need to save for a rainy day if funds already on hand will take care of a deluge. Thus, we should expect to find some difference in the expenditure patterns of two persons who work side by side if one of them had inherited a substantial sum.

When we step outside the rather narrow confines of inheritance and windfall profits, the case is not so clear. If a family saves for some future goal, we should not expect the successful fulfillment of its program to lessen future efforts. If a program calls for saving $500 each year for 30 years—in order to provide, say, a retirement fund—naturally, the stock of assets will grow. We should not expect this growth to lessen future saving.

But statistics of consumer expenditure indicate that assets do affect saving. At every income level, we observe lower average saving (higher consumption) for those who possess assets than for those who do not. An alternative explanation is that the assets make it easier to dis-save. Those without assets must borrow; those with assets merely use them for consumption and can, if they choose, overspend their income. For this reason, we should expect to find a higher proportion of dis-savers among asset-holders. These dis-savers lower the average saving for the entire group. It is not so clear that asset-holding alters the amount of saving by those who actually save.

In Chapter 12, we shall discuss the *Pigou effect,* which is concerned with the effect of price changes upon consumer spending. If the general price level changes, consumers should revalue their assets in terms of the new purchasing power. Some of these assets, especially stocks and other equity investments, will change with the price level; and their purchasing power will consequently be unaffected. Those assets that are measured in purely monetary terms, such as bonds or bank deposits, will remain fixed in dollars. Their purchasing power will therefore fall if prices rise and rise if prices fall.

Assuming that consumers revalue their assets in this fashion, we should expect a fall in the price level to increase the consumption function, since the money assets have increased in value. This reaction plays an important part in analyzing the reaction of the economy to price changes. We shall discuss it in more detail in Chapter 12.

Although we have been discussing only consumer assets, consumer debt is analogous in its effects. One would expect to find that consumers with relatively large debts tend to consume less, for they work to pay off the debts. All the other effects can be similarly analyzed, with consumer debt playing the role of negative consumer assets. Thus, larger debt should have the same effect as smaller assets.

Tastes and Habits

The ultimate goal of consumption is to provide satisfaction (or utility) to the consumer. One would therefore imagine that it would be appropriate to include some measure of satisfaction in the consumption function. Unfortunately, no simple measure of taste exists. The usual way of avoiding this dilemma is to assume that consumers' tastes do not change radically from year to year. Such an assumption is more acceptable in our discussion of total consumption than it would be if we were discussing consumption of individual items. All we need assume is that the satisfaction people derive from consumption now and the satisfaction to be derived from future consumption (saving) change together. As medical progress increases the expected length of life and the years to live on assets, we should expect some change in this preference, but such change takes place slowly. It is therefore ignored in most discussions of the consumption function.

It is sometimes suggested that one should include consumers' *needs,* as opposed to mere taste, in the consumption function. In this sense, one might include some measure of the cost of necessities—food, clothing, and housing. Such a measure is not easily definable, since necessities mean different things to different people. Does "necessary" housing mean a tent, a shack, or a Park Avenue apartment? What kind of clothing is "necessary"? What kind of food? In one divorce case, the wife listed the necessary expenses for herself and her child as $3500 per month. An adequate diet with all essential food elements can be provided for less than half the amount that the average family spends. In view of this wide range of definition, economists have been unable to give any objective meaning to the term *necessity.*

Since tastes tend to harden into habits, several attempts have been made to introduce this habit structure into the consumption function. The simplest way of including it is to use an average of the income of the preceding few years as well as present income. The higher the previous income, the more one would consume *now,* whatever the level of current income. Another way of including past history is to use the highest previous income. Such a formulation assumes that people try to maintain high consumption standards but not low ones. Although neither of these measures is ideal, either will serve as an index to measure the continuity of consumption patterns.

Short and Long Run

One anomaly of consumption behavior which has been observed in the United States is the inconsistency between results obtained from study of different lengths of time. The longest series covers the period since 1869. These data seem to indicate that consumption has been fairly steady at 90 percent of income (that is, that a is zero and that the marginal propensity to consume is about 0.90). If, on the other hand, data covering a shorter period are used, a positive a is found and a marginal propensity to consume nearer 0.80. This latter result holds true whether the data used are for the prewar period 1929 to 1941 or the postwar period since 1947. If the two periods are combined, a drop in a and a rise in the marginal propensity to consume is found.

Many explanations have been offered. One possibility is that the short-run consumption function is really relatively flat (as shown in Figure 4.1), but that it slowly drifts upward over time. Such an upward drift, if viewed over a long period of time, would give the impression of a single, steep consumption function when in fact there may be several separate functions, each of which is comparatively flat. Such a possibility is shown in Figure 6.2, where the three functions, C_1, C_2, and C_3, represent three separate short-run functions and the circles on them represent individual years. If one were to fit a single line to these points, it would look more like C_L: that is, it would appear steeper and would seem to be intersecting the origin. This impression would be further increased if one used averages of, say, five-year periods instead of single years.

Several likely explanations can be given for the upward drift of consumption. There is the shift of population from farms to cities, and most studies indicate that the marginal propensity to consume is lower for farmers than for city dwellers. It is also known that consumer tastes and habits are affected by the spending of those around them. Thus, the rise in income generally tends to increase the consumption behavior even of those whose incomes remain constant. This same process transforms luxuries into necessities, thereby increasing the consumption function. New products tend to encourage this upward drift of consumption. Notice that the inclusion of past incomes in the consumption function which was suggested in the last section is, in effect, a way to allow for the upward drift of consumption.

Another possible explanation of the upward drift is the importance of consumer assets. The general rise in incomes over the last century has been accompanied by a general rise in consumer liquid assets. If asset-holding encourages greater spending out of current income, one would observe an upward drift in the consumption function.

A closely related explanation of the discrepancy between long- and short-run behavior is also based upon habit patterns. If income moves up slowly, one expects consumption to rise almost proportionately. However, if income then declines, consumers might try to maintain the standard of living previously achieved, so that the marginal propensity to consume moving downward would be comparatively low. This low marginal propensity to consume would also apply during the recovery until such time as the old level of income is passed. Such behavior, as shown in Figure 6.3, would lead to results similar to those of Figure 6.2. However, it is usually described as a *ratchet* effect in contrast to the *drift* effect previously considered. To allow for such behavior, one would use the previous high income as an

Consumption Drift

FIGURE 6.2

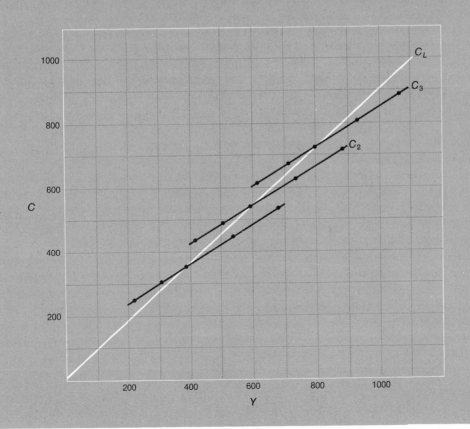

Consumption Ratchet

FIGURE 6.3

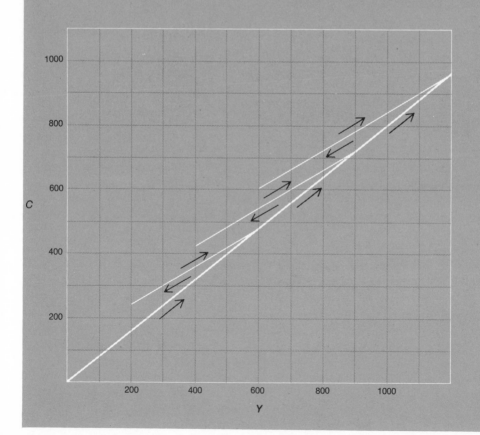

index of the standard of living already achieved. This formulation, introduced by James Duesenberry, is similar to that given in the last section and, like it, depends upon the development of consumption habits.

Permanent Income

Although the most easily obtainable measure of income may be disposable income, many theoretical considerations suggest that it is not the best guide to consumer behavior. If an individual received a windfall in one year, one would hardly expect him to act the same as if that were his normal income. Similarly, an individual whose income is temporarily below *normal* might continue his regular consumption pattern. Such considerations suggest that one ought to distinguish between permanent and transitory income components. For example, a salesman whose commissions fluctuate between $6000 and $10,000 per year might consume as if his income were $8000 regardless of the actual amount earned in one year. Alternately, he might keep his purchases of nondurables and services fairly constant, but concentrate his durable purchases in the better years.

The use of the permanent-income hypothesis offers another explanation of the difference between long- and short-run behavior. While long-run growth presumably increases permanent income, business-cycle fluctuations represent only changes in transitory income. As a result, consumption reacts less to these latter changes than to more permanent ones.

To achieve the maximum precision, our estimates of a household's spending should probably be based on its entire expected income stream. This is especially important among professional and managerial families, who can reasonably expect their incomes to keep rising for many years. Such families often spend to the limit of their incomes while other families with much lower, but stable, incomes save a substantial portion.

Unfortunately, it has not been possible to give this distinction between permanent and transitory income its full weight in estimating consumption. The available statistical data do not make it possible to distinguish permanent income from measured income. Furthermore, it is not quite certain how consumers estimate their permanent income. How many "$10,000 years" would be required before the salesman in the example decides that his income is not $8000? At the present time, the permanent-income hypothesis has provided many useful insights, but it has not proved possible to give it full weight in statistical analysis because of the measurement difficulties.

Distribution *of* Income

If all consumers had exactly the same marginal propensity to consume, the redistribution of income from one man to another would decrease the consumption of one by exactly the amount it increased the consumption of the other. To the extent that the marginal propensity to consume differs from individual to individual, it would be possible to change the total consumption by such transfers. A transfer of $1000 from a man with a marginal propensity to consume of 0.50 to a man with a marginal propensity of 0.75 would increase total consumption by $250.

In the United States, there is some difference between high- and low-income groups in the marginal propensity to consume, but less than most people think. Casual observation tends to concentrate on the *average* propensity to consume, not the *marginal*. A poor man may spend all his income for consumption, but he will not necessarily spend all of any increase he receives. Table 6.1 lists consumption and income for average families in various income brackets. There is much less variation in the *marginal* propensity to consume than in the *average* propensity to consume. Since casual impressions are based upon the average propensity, they tend to be misleading. One estimate indicated that if all consumers had the average income, consumption would be 4 percent higher than it is under the present distribution. Moving each consumer halfway to the average would in-

TABLE 6.1

FAMILY INCOME AND CONSUMPTION, 1960[a]

Disposable Income	Consumption
$2000	$2200
4000	3900
6000	5550
8000	7050
10,000	8500
12,000	9900

[a] Derived from *Consumer Expenditures and Income*, Supplement 3–Part A to BLS Report 237–238 (Washington: U.S. Government Printing Office, July 1964), pp. 2–3. The data in the table refer to all urban families and single consumers.

crease consumption by 2½ percent.[1] These estimates indicate that the possibilities of increasing consumption by redistributing income are quite modest. (Although many left-wing British economists have advocated such a policy, very few American economists have done so.)

Even these increases probably overstate the effects of redistribution; they are computed on the assumption that each individual whose income changed would behave exactly like those who previously had such income. Such an assumption is tenable only if consumption of each individual is independent of that of other individuals. But consumption is not independent, for people try to keep up with the Joneses and ahead of the Smiths. If income were redistributed, those with lower incomes would find that the Joneses are not so hard to keep up with. Therefore, somewhat less consumption would be expected at each income level than before. Those who are trying to keep ahead of the Smiths will find their task more difficult, since the Smiths may also have more money now. Thus, it can be said

[1] See Harold Lubell, "Effects of Redistribution of Income on Consumers' Expenditures," *American Economic Review*, 37 (March 1947), pp. 157–170; and his "Correction," *American Economic Review*, 37 (December 1947), p. 930.

that the *Jones effect* would tend to reduce the gain in consumption caused by redistribution but that the *Smith effect* might tend to raise it. If one can judge by advertisers' concentration on emulation as a motive, it is probably true that the *Jones effect* is more important in the United States than elsewhere, but that the *Smith effect* may dominate in other countries. On this ground, redistribution of income, in the United States, at least, is not apt to lead to any great increase in consumption.

Another kind of redistribution may be of somewhat greater importance. It was previously noted that farm families consume less at each income level than urban families. There are also differences between saving ratios of the self-employed and wage earners (possibly associated with differing estimates of permanent income). These possibilities suggest that it might be desirable to reflect the distribution of income by type in our consumption function. One possibility would be to use several components of income, as in the following equation

$$C = a + b_1 Y_1 + b_2 Y_2 + b_3 Y_3 \tag{6.1}$$

In this case, Y_1 stands for wage and salary income; Y_2 for agricultural income; and Y_3 for property income. Some attempts at this type of division have been made with useful results. However, if the relations between types of income are reasonably stable or change smoothly over time, such detail is unnecessary.

Credit Terms

It was once common for economists to include the rate of bank interest as an important factor in determining consumption and saving—sometimes, indeed, as the only factor. These economists felt that the rate of interest was the price at which one bought future goods by giving up present goods. One would naturally expect that this price would affect the choice between present and future goods, just as any other price affects the amount purchased. But there was some confusion about the direction of this effect. If interest rates were higher, one could gain more by postponing purchase; however, one could obtain the same future goods for less present saving. (Those who are familiar with the theory of consumer choice will recognize an income effect and a substitution effect.) Whether one would save less or more as rates rose depended upon the relative strength of desires for present goods and future goods. The issue was never really settled.

This debate has now become largely academic in the United States. Years of low interest rates have tended to keep the rate from fluctuating very much. If, as many believe, the incentives toward greater and lesser saving almost cancel each other, then the effects of changes in the rate of interest will be slight. If, in addition, the changes are small, the interest rate can be dropped from the discussion of consumption and saving.

A second factor has also contributed to the decreased importance of the interest rate. In the eighteenth and nineteenth centuries, most saving was done by the richer classes. Many of these people had incomes largely derived from investments. They were naturally quite sensitive to changes in the interest rate. In modern America, smaller savers account for a large portion of saving. Even a man with an annual income of $10,000 may save about $1000 a year. On this sum he can earn, at 4 percent, only $40 annually. This return is less than $\frac{1}{2}$ of 1 percent of his annual income. It is difficult to imagine that he would react very much if the interest rate rose so that he would earn $50 instead of $40.

The increasing importance of durable consumer goods has given credit a new role in the analysis of consumer behavior. The previous discussion dealt with consumers as lenders; consumer durables have made them borrowers. Many durables are quite expensive and are, therefore, often purchased on credit. In some cases, the competition among sellers seems to revolve around liberalized credit terms rather than changed prices. The interest rate itself is seldom important in such calculations; many buyers do not even know the rate on their contracts. The terms of the loan are the important factors, especially the size of the downpayment and the period of the loan. During inflationary periods, the United States government caused a substantial decline in sales of such goods with credit regulations. On installment buying, these regulations usually required a 25-percent downpayment and payment of the balance within 18 months. Such regulations probably had more effect on buying than any reasonable change in interest rates. Similar effects have also been noted in housing, where the terms are often more important than the interest rate or even the price.

In summary, then, it can be said that interest rates have a relatively minor effect on saving and consumption, but that credit terms have an important effect on consumption, especially on the purchase of durable goods.

Population

The discussion of consumption by family groups gives a clue to the role of population in determining consumption. If a family has an income of $8000, it spends $7050 on consumption. If the same $8000 were given to two families, each receiving $4000, the total consumption would be $7800 or $3900 per family. It is clear, therefore, that the consumption function will be higher if a given income is shared among more people.

A similar effect can be noted from an examination of income and consumption data for families of varying size. Table 6.2 presents such comparisons. They indicate higher consumption in each income bracket by the larger families. For both these reasons, it is said that a larger population means a higher consumption function.

TABLE 6.2

FAMILY SIZE AND CONSUMPTION, 1960

Income	Family Consumption		
	2 persons	3 persons	4 persons
$ 1000–1999	$ 2043	$ 1998	$ 2145
2000–2000	2681	2842	3423
3000–3999	3653	3948	4279
4000–4999	4349	4731	4873
5000–5999	4776	5411	5616
6000–7499	5844	6364	6502
7500–9999	7000	7602	7635
10,000–14,999	8674	9834	10,183
15,000 and up	14,549	13,998	14,406

SOURCE: *Consumer Expenditures and Income*, Supplement 3–Part A to BLS Report 237–238 (Washington: U.S. Government Printing Office, July 1964), *passim*. The data in the table refer to urban families.

Government and Consumption

In the modern world, the government has come to play an increasingly important role in economic life. The influence of the government in the discussion of investment will be noted; its influence on consumption is comparable.

The largest single avenue of government influence is its effect on disposable income, which was previously defined as income minus taxes plus transfer payments. In 1967 transfers amounted to about 6 percent of GNP and taxes to about 29 percent. It is clear that changes in either taxes or transfers will affect consumption. In Chapter 5 these effects were analyzed and multipliers were computed to measure the magnitude of the change. If one wished, the analysis of Chapter 5 could be carried to greater lengths. It was previously noted that different families have different marginal propensities to consume. In particular, this propensity is higher in low-income groups and large families, lower in high-income groups and small families. A comprehensive study of the effects of tax changes would include the individuals whose taxes are being changed and would measure the marginal propensity to consume of these taxpayers. Such analysis often underlies political debate on tax change. One should distinguish also between excise taxes, which fall directly upon consumption, and income taxes, which fall upon consumption and saving equally. This distinction will not be made here, however, since these computations are meaningful only in relation to specific tax programs.

The consumption function ordinarily relates consumption to disposable income. The government activities discussed in the foregoing paragraph do not alter the consumption *function*; they change the *amount* of consumption by movement along the function. But other activities of the government do change the consumption function itself; that is, they alter the amount that will be consumed at each income level. Already mentioned is the role of credit terms in durable-goods consumption; government regulations can alter these terms. Many of the other regulatory activities of the government also affect consumption. Highway rules affect the demand for certain kinds of automobiles; building codes affect purchases of home furnishings. In a complex society with a widespread program of government activities, the list can be extended almost indefinitely.

Finally, the form of government expenditures bears an important relation to consumption. Many consumer goods have either a competitive or a complementary relationship to government expenditures.

New roads might increase the demand for automobiles; a better so-cial-security system may lessen the need for private saving. There are many examples of such relationships, but an estimate of the exact effect would require detailed analysis of the government budget.

The growth of government-saving programs may actually increase the total level of consumption in a society. In the typical case, such additional programs are accompanied by increased taxes. One might be inclined, therefore, to say that such programs merely transfer the saving act from the individual to the government. In some cases, however, the sum of costs for the government may be less than the sum of the costs for the individuals in the society. All are aware that one can often buy more retirement income from an insurance company than one could provide by saving the same amount of money. This is possible because many people do not live to collect this sum. All insurance works on this principle. An insurance company can insure a house against fire for a few dollars a year, because most houses do not burn down.

Some things are not insurable. Private companies can offer medical insurance because only some people get sick every year; they cannot offer unemployment insurance because too many policyholders would require payment at the same time. Only the government, with its almost unlimited credit and the power to create money, can offer such insurance. Over the long run this insurance can be self-supporting, but private companies might find themselves bankrupt in the early years.

For such items, in which the alternatives are private saving or government programs, the government program is apt to be cheaper. An individual must guard against the worst; the government can guard against the average. Because these programs contain an insurance element, their over-all cost may be less. It should be made clear that this saving exists *only* in cases in which private insurance companies cannot supply such coverage. Where coverage is available privately, one must compare the relative efficiency of the government and private companies.

A Statistical Consumption Function?

The previous discussions indicate that the analysis of consumption is a very complex matter. It is also one of the areas of economics which lends itself well to study by teams of specialists. The fields of economics, psychology, and sociology can all add to the under-standing of consumption behavior. Since few individual scholars have training in all these fields, the essential work must be done by group study, a relatively slow process. Inevitably, some have sought to short-cut this process by computing statistical consumption functions. This process consists of assuming that the relationship of the past will hold, at least approximately, into the future.

Two different techniques are used for this process, one based upon aggregate income and consumption, the other upon family-budget data. The first is quite simple—at least in principle. It consists of plotting national consumption against national disposable income, as in Figure 6.4, and drawing a line through these points. The details of such analysis can be found in any text on statistics. By the use of multiple regression, one can include other variables—for example, population or consumer assets—but the principles are similar. Further refinements are possible, including the adjusting of national data to a per capita basis and adjusting for prices.

There are two main disadvantages in such analysis. Most of the variables show a relatively steady increase from year to year. It is, therefore, very difficult to ascribe the proper proportion of change in consumption to the various causal factors. As seen earlier, many phenomena can be explained with either of several variables. For simple prediction, any one would be adequate if one were sure that these variables would continue to maintain their proportionality in the future. If only one increases, however, while others do not, one cannot be sure of the result.

This continued growth is the source of the other disadvantage. In many cases, the estimate for next year depends upon values of con-sumption and income which are beyond all previously observed values. In the historic case of this guessing game, many economists attempted during the latter part of World War II, to predict income and con-sumption in the postwar period. Since the war years were obviously distorted, such predictions were based on data for 1941 and earlier years. The highest consumption in that period was in 1941: $76.6 billion (measured in 1939 dollars). In 1946 consumption was $95.7 billion (still in 1939 dollars). The statisticians were trying to predict a consumption level 25 percent higher than any previously observed. It is not surprising that their efforts were not very successful.

The second form of statistical consumption function is based on consumer-budget studies, by assuming a changed distribution of in-come and assuming that each family will consume the same amount as those which previously had that income. Table 6.3 shows the aver-age disposable income and average consumption expenditure for fami-

Time-Series Consumption Function, 1929-1967

FIGURE 6.4

Source: Economic Report of the President. Washington, D.C.: U.S. Government Printing Office, 1968, p. 227.

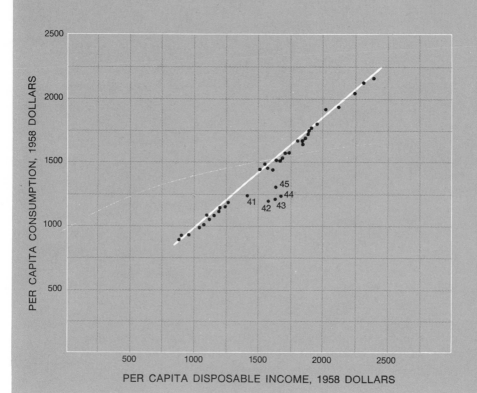

TABLE 6.3

INCOME AND CONSUMPTION, CHANGING
DISTRIBUTIONS

Income ($)	Mean Disposable Income ($)	Consumption ($)	Percentage Distribution of Families		
			Actual	10% increase	20% increase
0–999	738	1310	2.4	2.2	2.0
1000–1999	1578	1770	8.7	7.1	6.1
2000–2999	2557	2676	9.9	8.9	7.9
3000–3999	3563	3716	11.4	9.9	8.7
4000–4999	4637	4502	13.2	11.4	9.7
5000–5999	5582	5245	13.1	12.1	11.0
6000–7499	6781	6234	16.3	15.9	15.8
7500–9999	8621	7545	14.9	16.9	18.7
10,000–14,999	11,822	9761	7.7	11.0	13.7
15,000 and up	22,270	14,790	2.4	4.6	6.4

SOURCE: *Consumer Expenditures and Income*, Supplement
3–Part A to BLS Report 237–238 (Washington: U.S.
Government Printing Office, July 1964) pp. 2–3. Data refer
to urban families and single households, 1960.

lies in each income group. Also shown is the percentage of families
in each income bracket. If all incomes rose by 10 percent, the families
whose incomes are now between zero and $1000 would be spread
between zero and $1100. The next group would be spread between
$1100 and $2200. By interpolation, one can calculate how many families would be between each of the old limits after the change. Each
of these percentages is then multiplied by the average income and
consumption in each group to find the average income and consumption for all families under each distribution. (One can convert these
averages into total income and consumption by multiplying by the
total number of families.) The results provide a statistical consumption function like that shown in Figure 6.5.

Statistical Consumption Function Derived from Budget Studies

FIGURE 6.5

Source: Calculated from 1960 data on urban families and single households shown in Table 6.3

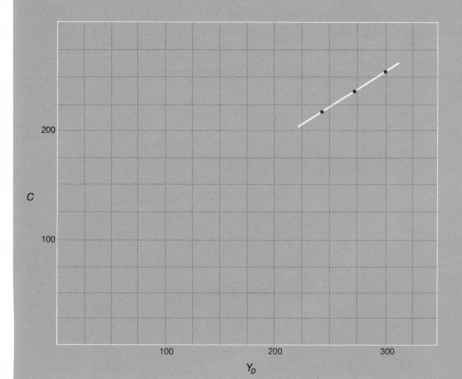

This process has not been as successful as estimation based on aggregate data. Considering the previous discussion of habits and relations of consumers, one would not expect consumers whose incomes move up proportionately to behave like those who previously had that income. Indeed, later studies seem to indicate that if all consumers move up together, each tends to save the same percentage of his income as *he* previously saved. This result is not sufficiently certain to permit prediction either, so this whole method has been substantially abandoned.

Most statistical studies of consumption in recent years have been very successful statistically, but less so economically. Correlation coefficients over 0.99 are common, even with the use of a few explanatory variables. However, none of these estimates gives a good indication of *changes* in consumption over short periods of time, such as a quarter. The rather dismal conclusion must be drawn that the consumption process is still not perfectly understood and that there is no substitute for full study. Statistics can be tremendously helpful in this study in verifying hypotheses and suggesting new ones, but correlation—no matter how sophisticated—is no substitute for a full study of causation.

PROBLEMS AND DISCUSSION QUESTIONS

1. If the purchase of consumer durables was treated as saving and depreciation on these durables as consumption, would you expect more or less change in consumption from year to year? Would you expect the consumption function to be steeper or flatter?

2. Much saving is now contractual—for example, in insurance policies. What effect does this have on the consumption function?

3. Habits of consumption have been introduced into the consumption function. Do you think saving habits might also be important? Which would matter more if incomes fell? If they rose?

4. What effect has the growth of hospitalization insurance had on the need for saving? On the consumption function?

5. (*For students with a background in statistics*) Enumerate some of the problems to be faced in estimating a consumption function by statistical methods.

SUGGESTED ADDITIONAL READINGS

There are very few general works on consumption and saving relations, but articles on specific studies or aspects abound.

Of these general books, one must mention James S. Duesenberry, *Income, Saving, and the Theory of Consumer Behavior* (Cambridge, Mass.: Harvard University Press, 1949). This volume explicitly introduced the social aspects of consumption and also indicated the role of previous income in determining current consumption. George Katona, *Psychological Aspects of Economic Behavior* (New York: McGraw-Hill, 1951) describes some aspects of the study of consumer behavior by survey techniques. The symposium *Savings in the Modern Economy*, Heller, Boddy, and Nelson, eds. (Minneapolis: University of Minnesota Press, 1953) discusses many aspects of saving and consumption behavior. Especially interesting is Chapter 13 by Duesenberry, Dorothy Brady, Imprie de Vegh, James Morgan, Margaret G. Reid, James Tobin, David McCord Wright, and Simon Kuznets.

The permanent income hypothesis was proposed in Milton Friedman, *A Theory of the Consumption Function* (Princeton, N.J.: Princeton University Press, 1957). However, see the comments of Margaret Reid in the Minnesota symposium as a forerunner. The use of lifetime average income was proposed in Franco Modigliani and Richard Brumberg, "Utility Analysis and the Consumption Function: An Interpretation of Cross-Section Data," in *Post-Keynesian Economics*, K. Kurihara, ed. (New Brunswick, N. J.: Rutgers University Press, 1954), pp. 388–436. This argument is closely related to the use of average past income for aggregate functions in Franco Modigliani, "Fluctuations in the Saving-Income Ratio: A Problem in Economic Forecasting," in *Studies in Income and Wealth*, 11 (New York: National Bureau of Economic Research, 1949), 371–441. *See also* Albert Ando and Franco Modigliani, "The 'Life Cycle' Hypothesis of Saving: Aggregate Implications and Tests," *American Economic Review* vol. 53 (1963) and their "Correction" a year later.

The use of income segments is proposed in L. R. Klein and A. S. Goldberger, *An Econometric Model of the United States, 1929–1952* (Amsterdam: North Holland, 1955).

On the role of asset-holdings *see* James Tobin, "Asset Holdings and Spending Decisions," *American Economic Review, Papers and Proceedings,* vol. 42 (1952).

On the effects of income redistribution, *see* the article by Lubell referred to footnote 1, this chapter.

Reviews of the consumption literature include L. R. Klein, "The Empirical Foundations of Keynesian Economics," *in* Kurihara, pp. 277–295; E. E. Hagen, "The Consumption Function," *Review of Economics and Statistics,* vol. 37 (1955); and Robert Ferber, "Research on Household Behavior," *American Economic Review,* vol. 52 (1962).

Much of the recent work on consumer behavior has been a part of the development of large-scale econometric models. *See,* for example, J. S. Duesenberry, Gary Fromm, L. R. Klein, and Edwin Kuh, eds., *The Brookings Quarterly Econometric Model of the United States* (Chicago: Rand McNally, 1965). Part III deals with consumption.

7

𝒯𝒽𝑒 Demand for Investment

In the simplified model of Chapters 4 and 5, investment was treated as an exogenous variable. In the chapters that follow, we will wish to treat it endogenously, that is, to build it into the model. We must therefore consider what determines the level of investment expenditure, including both those influences that will be part of our models and those that will remain exogenous.

Throughout this discussion, it is well to remember that investment for the whole society consists only in new physical goods to be used in further production. If one individual buys securities from another individual, his investment is counteracted by the other man's sale. If the individual purchases newly issued stock, he merely transfers his money to a corporation, receiving from the corporation a claim against its future income. Only when the corporation uses this money to buy buildings, machinery, or inventories has any real investment taken place. We are therefore discussing the problems of the corporate manager, not of the stockholder.

In a simple sense, the problem of investment is trivial: a businessman will make any investment if he and his backers think it will be profitable. To examine the problems of determining profitability, let us consider the problem of a firm trying to decide whether to purchase a specific asset—say, a truck to be used for commercial hauling. The firm can expect, for each year it owns the truck, to receive certain fees for hauling. We may refer to these fees, over the years, as a *stream of revenues*. If the truck is expected to have a salvage value, that value can be added to the last revenue in the stream. The firm must also expect to incur each year a number of out-of-pocket costs, for taxes, gasoline, oil, tires, wages of truck drivers, and all the other expenses of doing business. Let us call these a *stream of costs*. The difference between these streams of revenues and costs constitutes a *stream of net returns* for the truck.

Against these net returns, spread through future years, the firm must match the original cost of the truck. It is obvious that these net returns must cover the depreciation on the truck. A moment's reflection, however, indicates that the stream of net revenues must also cover the cost of financing the original purchase. If a firm borrows money for such a purchase, it must pay interest; if it uses its own money, it must forego alternative opportunities. For the sake of simplicity, let us assume that the firm borrows the money. It is then meaningful to ask: At what interest rate could it borrow money to buy the truck and still break even? In more formal terms, this question becomes: What interest rate makes the present value of the return equal to the purchase price? If this interest rate (called the *yield*) is greater than the market interest rate at which it must borrow, the firm would buy the truck. (Numerical details of computing the yield are given in the Appendix to this chapter.)

The yield on an investment is called the *marginal efficiency of capital*. It is called *efficiency* because it indicates a *rate* of net return over costs; it is called *marginal* because it refers only to additions to total capital, not to the yield of existing capital assets. (Even though the return on an existing railroad may be 30 percent, the return on a second railroad planned to serve the same towns might be very low, or even negative.)

If we imagine similar computations for every businessman who contemplates making an investment, we can conceive a marginal-efficiency-of-capital schedule for the entire society. We assume, of course, that different firms do not contemplate making the same investment. Thus there could be, at a given time, $30-billion worth of projects yielding 20 percent or more, $8-billion worth yielding 19 percent, and $8-billion worth yielding 18 percent. So, adding, one can compute the number of projects yielding as much as, or more than, a given return. In the example above, there are $38 billion yielding 19 percent or more, $46 billion yielding 18 percent, and so on. Such a tabulation is shown in Figure 7.1.

We would expect businessmen to make whatever investments they can find which yield more than the market rate of interest. We can

Hypothetical Marginal Efficiency *of* Capital

FIGURE 7.1

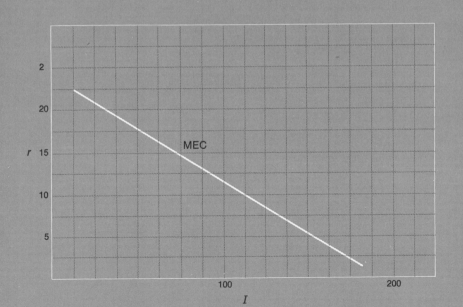

The Determinants of Investment

FIGURE 7.2

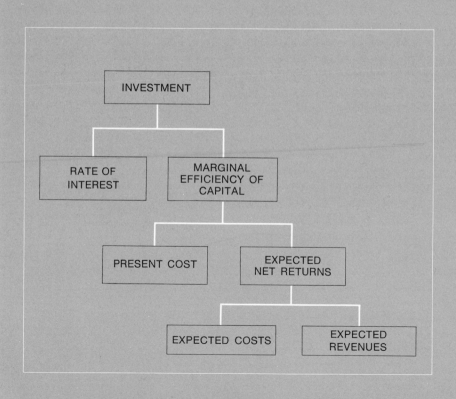

therefore turn the marginal-efficiency-of-capital schedule around and make it an investment-demand schedule. From Figure 7.1, we learn that there is $110 billion worth of investment with a marginal efficiency greater than 10 percent. It therefore follows that the demand for investment at a market interest rate of 10 percent is $110 billion. Since the marginal-efficiency-of-capital schedule enables us to find the demand for investment if we know the rate of interest, we say that investment is a *function* of the rate of interest. (Remember the definition of a function given in Chapter 1.) If we knew the form of this function, we could state it algebraically and include it in the system of Chapter 5, just as we did the consumption function. Unfortunately we do not know this form and must be contented with the general form

$$I = f(r) \tag{7.1}$$

to indicate that investment is a function of the rate of interest. (Read this equation as "I equals f of r", not "f times r.")

The principles of investment given here do not change if we relax our assumption that all investments are made with borrowed money. We should not expect businessmen to invest their own funds in projects that yield less than the market rate of interest, for they have other, more profitable uses for their money. The factors that affect investment are summarized in Figure 7.2.

We have focused our initial attention upon the rate of interest because we will want to include interest as an endogenous variable within our more complicated models. However, other factors are probably more responsible for changes in investment than changes in interest rates; in other words, *shifts* in the schedule are more important than movements *along* it. We must therefore turn our attention to other factors.

The Declining Demand for Investment

Consumption is a continuing process, so that it is reasonable to assume a consumption function that is relatively unchanged from year to year. Investment demand is self-destroying, so that the investment function is always different in succeeding years.

Marginal Efficiency of Capital, Successive Periods

FIGURE 7.3

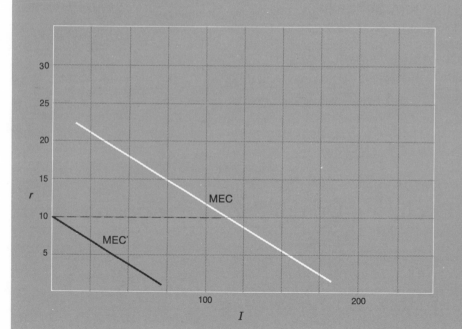

The reason for the change is the very nature of investment, which is the purchase of new capital goods. If a society had all of the capital goods required to produce its national product in one year and then wished to produce the same quantities of the same goods the following year, no net investment would be required. (Replacements of worn-out capital would still be necessary.)

We find the same result by looking at the marginal-efficiency-of-capital schedule. In the schedule of Figure 7.1, we saw that there were $110 billion worth of investments that yielded over 10 percent. If the market rate of interest were 10 percent, investment of $110 billion would be made. If nothing else changed the marginal efficiency schedule for the following year would contain only the lower half of the previous schedule and would look like the curve in Figure 7.3. Notice that there are now no investments with yields over 10 percent; all of them have been made. If the market rate of interest remained unchanged, investment in the new period would be zero. In order to keep investment at the previous level, it would be necessary to find new opportunities which had not existed before. The study of investment is therefore the study of change.

Expectations

The marginal efficiency of capital is the yield that makes the present value of expected net returns equal to the purchase price. The net returns are obtained by subtracting future costs from future revenues. Therefore the marginal efficiency of any investment can be altered by changing one of the three components: purchase price, future revenues, and future costs.

Two of these three are estimates of the future. Since these items can seldom be determined objectively, the expectations of businessmen for the future are very important. If businessmen feel generally optimistic, they will estimate future revenues high and future costs low, with a correspondingly high marginal efficiency of capital. If they feel pessimistic, the marginal efficiency of capital will be low. This influence is so important that entire theories of income variation have been built upon "waves of optimism and pessimism." Occasionally some astrologer-turned-economist chooses to find a relation between these moods and cosmic rays, sunspots, or other radiations from outer space. Novelists sometimes give the impression that these attitudes (and the expectations derived from them) stem from the business-man's reaction to a case of indigestion or to a pleasant smile from his wife at the breakfast table. Such economic studies of the invest-ment process as are available indicate that most business expectations are made of much more substantial stuff. They result from engineering studies, market surveys, analysis of economic trends, and other such research. The importance of such research as compared with subjective factors has been indicated on several occasions, when executive opinion surveys reported that the average businessman expected a general recession but that he was still planning new investments "because our firm is different." Apparently the research data for his firm in-fluenced his decisions more than his impressions of the economy. Investment decisions have not yet been reduced to a simple routine within the capabilities of ordinary clerks, but they are far removed from the area of whim and superstition.

Any analysis of the future usually starts with the conditions of the present. In the absence of any concrete evidence that a change should be expected, businessmen will assume that the conditions of the present will continue into the future. This statement is, of course, obvious, but it underscores the fact that changes will determine the *deviations from the present*. Thus, a businessman who is trying to estimate his future labor costs must begin with a knowledge of the labor-union strength in his firm, in his industry, and in the country at large. From these data, he can estimate whether the general trend of wages in his firm will be similar to that in the rest of the country or not. Similarly, if he is trying to estimate the tax costs for his firm, he will generally start with the present level of taxes and modify this level by prospective changes in the structure. In cases where there is a customary rate of change, it is probably that trend which is projected into the future, not the present level. For example, no businessman would expect future wages to be the same as present ones.

It is also worthwhile to remind ourselves that the future returns involved cover a series of time periods in the future. It is demonstrated in the Appendix that marginal efficiency is the yield (r) which makes

$$Q = \frac{R_1}{(1+r)^1} + \frac{R_2}{(1+r)^2} + \frac{R_3}{(1+r)^3} + \cdots \atop + \frac{R_n}{(1+r)^n} \tag{7.2}$$

where Q is the purchase price and $R_1, R_2, R_3, \ldots, R_n$ are the re-turns in successive years. In a stationary world, all the R's would be equal, but in our own changing world they are apt to be quite different. Many businessmen fear that new products and new processes from other firms may make the investment that seems desirable today quite unprofitable at some time in the future. The usual way to allow for this possibility is to lower the R's for later years to allow for the increased probability that competition may cut future revenues. The early returns are probably quite safe, since most businesses have an idea of what their competition will be in the near future, but returns for later years are usually cut down to allow for the unknown.

One must keep in mind that the impact of a change that affects only one term—say, R_3—is quite different from the impact of a change that affects them all. We must guard against the casual tendency to act as if all the R's were identical.

An example will make this distinction clearer. In 1953, Congress extended the excess-profits tax on corporations for one year. The tax duly expired on January 1, 1954. At the time of the extension, dire results were predicted on the ground that this tax lowered returns so much that investment would be unprofitable. Such an assumption was probably unwarranted. Even if an investment could be made with no time lag, only the first year's return would be affected by the tax. On a 20-year investment which yields 8 percent, cutting the first year's return to *zero* would lower the yield only to 7 percent. Since the tax did not erase the return completely, this change is an overestimate of its effects. If the investment took some time in construction, the tax extension might expire without altering any of the returns, for the new investment might not produce before January 1, 1954.

In view of the rather slight effects indicated above, why were there such catastrophic predictions? One might attribute the argument to pure propaganda or to businessmen's traditional dislike for taxes. More probably, the answer lies in the failure to distinguish between a decline in R_1, the return for the first year, and all the R's of the stream. It is true that a permanent extension of the excess-profits tax would have caused a substantial decline in the marginal efficiency of capital; it is not true that a short temporary extension would have that effect.

In fairness to the opponents of this tax, there is one important argument against even a temporary extension. Businessmen might feel that a temporary extension could be followed by another temporary extension and thus become, in fact, permanent. Looking back, we can see that the congressmen who voted for the extension had no such intention. But businessmen are not mind readers. They must guess the intention from the action and might infer an intention to make the tax permanent. If the extension creates such an expectation among businessmen, then, in fact, all R's are lowered and the predicted results occur.

The succeeding sections of this chapter discuss some elements that affect these expectations, as well as certain other factors affecting the marginal efficiency of capital. These objective factors do not, however, explain everything. There always remains a degree of uncertainty stemming from the estimation of some uncontrolled variables. The uncertainty about the permanence of the tax extension discussed above is one such case, but there are many others. These uncertainties explain the popularity among businessmen of those periodicals that claim to predict future trends. It also explains the increasing competition among "Washington newsletters," which concentrate on government developments. These uncertainties also account for the fact that the analysis of investment is one of the least satisfactory aspects of economic theory.

Indicators

Although investments are made only on the strength of expectations, both businessmen and economists continually search for current measures that will serve as a clue to future profitability. Businessmen need such indicators for their own decisions; economists need them for forecasts. As expected, no indicator works very well, but there are several that provide clues.

The best indicator of future investment is profits. One knows from the usual economic theory of the firm that rising profits are the society's signal for the expansion of an industry. When profits are high, firms can usually expand their production facilities and increase profits still further. It is always possible that firms in an industry have some reason for believing that the increased profits are temporary, but in the absence of such a reason there would seem to be room for new investment.

A second indicator is the sales of the industry. We shall see in a later section that many industries tend to maintain a certain ratio between capital and output. An expansion of sales, therefore, indicates an expansion of capital, that is, new investment. Again, however, the expansion of sales must be expected to be permanent.

A third indicator, closely related to the last, is capacity. In those industries where capacity is defined, a certain rate of utilization is considered normal. If *normal* means 90 percent of capacity, we would certainly not expect new investment to be undertaken when the industry is operating at 70 percent, but would expect it when operations rise to 95 percent.

In using all these indicators, there is a question of timing. The process of investment takes time. Executives must decide that additional facilities are needed; plans must be made and discussed with various operating personnel; and approved by the appropriate boards and committees; bids must be solicited; and construction begun and completed. On some major plant investment this process may take years; on inventory accumulations only days; various kinds of equipment may take any period in between. Caution is needed, therefore, when one considers what indicators are appropriate for a given investment. Profits in 1965 might lead to an inventory build-up in 1965, to new equipment in 1966, and to new plants in 1967 or 1968. The analysis of these lags is often a very important part of the analysis of business-cycle movements.

Innovation

New techniques, processes, and products have always been important stimuli to investment. Many business-cycle theories have placed their main emphasis on the role these new developments have played in promoting investment. An innovation is the introduction of any of these new elements into the economic process. It therefore usually requires investment because processes and techniques are often built into the capital structure of a plant. (Imagine trying production-line assembly of automobiles in a commercial garage, or custom building on an assembly line.) In many cases, a new product requires new machinery for processing it. Thus innovation and investment usually go hand in hand.

The impetus to such investment can be traced to the lowering of costs or the increase in revenues. Unless a new product produces more revenue than any of the existing products, it remains merely an invention, one more model and set of plans to clutter the files of the U.S. Patent Office. Only when the prospective revenue from a new product is high does the invention find its way into the economic process and become an innovation. Similarly, new production techniques are adopted only if they are more efficient and therefore cheaper than existing methods. Thus we can say that the marginal efficiency of capital is increased by a steady flow of new innovations.

The foregoing summary presents only half the picture. It is true that innovation increases the marginal efficiency of capital for the innovator. It is also true that it causes the marginal efficiency of capital to fall for the older firms. (Imagine what must have happened to the marginal efficiency of capital in the buggy industry during the early years of the twentieth century.) In some cases, the fear of competition from products yet unborn may decrease the marginal efficiency. If a given industry has a record of innovation which demonstrates that new developments will make the old methods obsolete about every five years, then a firm contemplating a new investment might well set R_6, R_7, and so forth all equal to zero, indicating that it can expect nothing after the fifth year. Such circumstances might actually lower the marginal efficiency.

The net effect of these two forces is usually in the direction of a higher marginal efficiency of capital. Only if the innovating firm makes its investment will there be a depressing effect on older firms. It is therefore clear that there must be at least some force in the direction of a higher marginal efficiency. Sometimes the new innovation can even appear without disturbing older firms at all, especially if the economy is growing. Only in the case of capital-saving innovations is it possible for the net effect to be a decrease. In such a case, where the capital-output ratio is lower for the new technique than for the old, the investment foregone might exceed the investment made. Even this effect is not inevitable. The old methods may be embodied in existing capital, which would not have required investment anyway. Thus the smaller amount of new capital nevertheless requires some net new investment. We may therefore be reasonably confident that innovation leads to a higher marginal efficiency of capital.

National Growth

As a society expands its markets expand with it. Such expansion, of course, leads to an increase in expected revenues, which in turn causes a rise in the marginal efficiency of capital. Thus, population growth and the development of new territories were an important factor in the high marginal efficiency of capital in the United States in the nineteenth century. Similarly, the increase in births in the

United States during the 1940s has been hailed as an insurance against depression, for it causes an increase in the marginal efficiency of capital.

We have already noted the importance of innovation in increasing the marginal efficiency of capital. Most investments, however, represent not innovations but, rather, expansion of facilities already in existence. It is important to exploit new processes and techniques—to produce electricity from atomic energy, gasoline from shale, and steel from low-grade iron ore. Quantitatively, these innovations are overshadowed by simple expansion—more steel mills, more diesel locomotives, more oil refineries. Probably the most important single factor in the expansion of these older forms of investment is the general expansion of markets in a growing society.

In the past, population growth increased the marginal efficiency of capital in another way: through its effect on expected future costs. An expanding population increases the labor supply, with a normal tendency to depress wages. Lower expected labor costs, by increasing expected net returns, increase the marginal efficiency of capital. Such factors may have been important in the nineteenth century when immigration and a high birth rate were swelling our population. Their importance in the United States of the twentieth century is lessened by decreased immigration and by increased unionization. The effect is mentioned here only as a sidelight on economic history.

Stagnation

The decade of the 1930s was a period of widespread unemployment in most countries. In the United States and England, many economists considered this unemployment a sign of vanishing investment opportunity. They argued that most of the best opportunities had already been exploited and that investment would not be sufficient to guarantee full employment. As a solution, they proposed that the government undertake a long-run policy of deficit spending to ensure full use of our resources. They also suggested certain programs to increase the consumption function, in order to reduce the amount of intended saving.

This argument had several facets. The first was the passing of the frontier. There no longer were any uninhabited territories to be settled and developed. The United States had less need for railroads and the purely physical marketing facilities which make settlements into towns and territories into states. Second, it seemed that the population of the United States would increase more slowly in the future. Throughout the 1920s and 1930s, although the population was still rising, the birth rate fell steadily. There would consequently be less need for *additional* housing and *additional* facilities to produce consumer goods, although the replacement demand would continue. Finally, the nineteenth and early twentieth century were periods of unprecedented technological change. Railroads, petroleum, steel, chemicals, automobiles, and electrical equipment were among the industries that grew during this period. There were grave doubts that such a pace could be maintained, much less exceeded. Since the other factors indicated less investment, technological change must provide all the more opportunities for investment and there was no evidence that it would do so.

The arguments for and against the stagnation thesis raged without any solution. A precise answer is impossible, by the nature of the problem, for this is economic "crystal-ball gazing" of the greatest magnitude. Even now, 30 years later, it is difficult to come to any firm conclusion. The "baby boom" of the 1940s and 1950s has lessened the impact of the population argument, but has slackened in the 1960s. The territorial argument remains intact. Technological progress continues, but comparison of rates is extremely unprecise. The history of the years since World War II can be cited on both sides. Stagnationists point out that we have maintained reasonably full employment only by large-scale government spending. It is true that the spending was undertaken for other reasons, but it can be argued that it prevented a major depression. The recessions of 1948, 1954, and 1958 took place despite large government budgets. Opponents charge that private investment and consumption would have filled the gap if it had not been for the repressive effects of the high taxes required by large government programs. Even today, fears of what would happen "if peace breaks out" indicate that the stagnation argument is not dead.

Old Capital and New Investment

Just as innovation may have a depressing effect on expansion of older methods, so the existence of old capital depresses the marginal efficiency for new investments. Other things being equal, the more capital in existence, the lower the marginal efficiency of capital. This is true because the old capital has presumably been invested in the most profitable enterprises, leaving the poorer ones unexploited. The heavy-traffic railroads have been built, leaving less profitable spur lines for the future. The existing firms in the automobile industry quite well blanket the range of consumer preferences, leaving only the luxury custom business or the low-priced small car for the newcomer.

Lest this sound too much like the complaint of Alexander the Great that there are no new worlds to conquer, let us hasten to add that other things are never equal. In the process of building an industry, all the good opportunities within that industry may be exploited, but often entire new industries are developed to complement it. No large railroads have been built in the United States in the twentieth century; the nineteenth century built them all. But many twentieth-century factories have been built because the nineteenth-century railroads provided suitable transportation facilities. Similarly, the automobile industry has no need for another General Motors; the society, however, needs good turnpike builders. Although many good opportunities have already been pre-empted in societies like the United States—more than in societies like India—unexplored projects still exist for future development. This is partly because there are more investment avenues to be explored in an industrial society and partly because the act of growth engenders more possibilities of growth. Our continued investment in the past has built up our capital-goods industries, which are themselves outlets for investment.

Old capital is also very important in another sense. The possibility of using the ratio of operations to capacity as an indicator of new investment was previously discussed. Such a ratio is based upon the idea that businesses will try to maintain a certain ratio between capital equipment and output. This same logic can be developed even further.

Suppose that there is a desired capital stock appropriate to every level of output. Normally, the actual stock will not be the same as this desired stock. This difference between desired and actual may be thought of as a capital gap. If an industry is growing, this gap usually will be positive and new investment will be required; if the industry is declining, the firm will tend to let its equipment wear out without replacement.

If businessmen were sure that the new level of output was permanent and that there were no capacity problems in the capital-goods industry, they would probably invest the full amount of the gap. In the absence of such certainty, they are apt to invest some portion of it, keeping some margin as their protection against a future decline.

It can then be said that investment is equal to some portion of the difference between desired capital stocks and existing stocks. (A similar principle for purchase of durable-consumer goods was discussed in Chapter 6, but as was indicated, there was difficulty in applying it there. Economists have been somewhat more successful in applying it to investment.)

The Accelerator

In business-cycle literature, it is common to emphasize the principle of the accelerator, a simplified version of the capital-stock adjustment principle. This principle states that new investment tends to be proportional to the change in consumption (or income). A numerical example will make this concept clear. Let us suppose that machines of a certain type turn out 100 units of product per day and that current production is 10,000 units per day. Then one hundred machines will be required. If the machines last for 20 years, the normal replacement demand for these machines will be five machines per year.

Let us assume that next year the demand for this product increases by 10 percent. This means 11,000 units of product per day, requiring one hundred and ten machines. Therefore, in addition to the usual replacement demand of five machines, there will be a demand for ten new machines to handle the additional demand for 1000 units. Thus, a 10-percent increase in demand can cause a 200-percent increase in investment. If demand had remained the same, investment would have been only for replacement. Thus, the accelerator places the emphasis on these changes in demand, not on their absolute level.

This theory is rather appealing, but an examination of the necessary conditions indicates that it is not very realistic. First of all, the theory assumes no unused capacity. If the firm described above already had one hundred twenty machines and were using only one hundred, one would not expect any increase in investment from a modest increase in demand. Therefore, the accelerator will not operate in a depression, which is characterized by excess capacity. Second, the accelerator assumes a fixed ratio between capital and output. This assumption is occasionally justified, but most firms can substitute labor for capital, at least within a limited range. Therefore, the investment process is more complicated than is indicated by the accelerator. Finally, even if these other conditions are fulfilled, businesses will purchase the new machines only if the demand is expected to remain high for the life of the machine. We have already mentioned some of the difficulties that arise when the first year's return, (R_1), is used as the basis for determining the return for all later years. To imagine that businessmen always make this simple assumption is to attribute to them a degree of naïvete that few of them possess.

For those who prefer empirical proof or disproof of these principles, we may say that the attempted statistical demonstrations of the accelerator have been remarkably unconvincing.

Even though we reject the simple version, the accelerator, like the more general capital-stock adjustment theory, does afford a clue to certain features of the investment process. Given the amount of old capital in existence, a rising national income tends to mean a higher marginal efficiency.

Purchase Price

The marginal efficiency of capital equates the present value of expected returns with the purchase price of the new investment goods. All the factors that we have been discussing affect the expected returns; the time has now come to consider the purchase price.

Unlike future revenues, the purchase price has an objective reality. It can be obtained either by consulting a catalogue or by asking contractors for bids. It is therefore not subject to the whims of the estimator but reflects cost and market conditions in the capital-goods industries.

Every technical advance in the capital-goods industries increases the marginal efficiency of capital in other industries. Similarly, increases in costs in the capital-goods industries lower the marginal efficiency of capital in all other industries. This relationship explains, at least partly, the great interest throughout the society in the wage negotiations of the steel industry and in the depletion of our iron mines.

Capital-goods industries are not exempt from the law of diminishing returns. If the demand for investment goods is very high, capital-goods firms will be working near capacity levels. As this level of operations is reached inefficiencies creep in and costs rise. Therefore, the marginal efficiency of capital, which is a demand for investment, is lowered when a high level of investment actually takes place.

In addition to the purely technical cost factors in the capital-goods industries, the degree of competition is also quite important. The greater the degree of monopoly in an industry, the higher will be the actual purchase price of capital goods. Such market monopoly in the capital-goods area is probably less dangerous than it would be in a consumer industry. Most firms that buy investment goods are well informed on possible alternative sources of supply; many are large enough to provide such alternatives themselves. In such a case, the competitiveness of the market is measured not by the number of firms but by all the *potential* alternatives.

Government and Investment

In the modern world, no form of economic activity escapes the influence of government. The marginal efficiency of capital is affected by many forms of government activity.

The most obvious influence is through taxation. Higher taxes either increase costs or decrease revenues, in both cases lowering the marginal efficiency of capital. Sales taxes lead to lower gross revenue, payroll and property taxes to increased costs. Corporation income taxes directly reduce the net return, the difference between revenues and costs. Even personal income taxes have their effect on the marginal efficiency, for they reduce sales and therefore diminish expected revenues.

There is one form of taxation which would not have such adverse effects upon investment. This would be a tax on pure economic profit—that is, a tax on the return above all costs, both explicit and implicit. Such a tax would be designed to lower the marginal efficiency of any profitable investment to a point just above the going rate of interest. For example, if the current rate of interest were 6 percent and a given investment, after allowance for risk, yielded 10 percent, the projected tax would reduce the yield on this investment *almost* to 6 percent. In such a case, the level of investment would not be affected. Unfortunately, such a tax is not administratively possible. No one has ever been able to construct a tax that is capable of objective determination and that lowers the yield on 10-percent investments to 6 percent without at the same time lowering the yield on 7-percent investments to 5 percent. All our present "profits" taxes are levied in part upon elements that are in actuality costs. The present corporate income tax, for example, does not allow deduction of interest on the money provided by stockholders. Therefore all present taxes lower, in varying degree, the marginal efficiency of capital.

The influence of government on the marginal efficiency does not end with taxes; government expenditures can also have an important effect. If these expenditures are apt to be competitive with business output, expected revenues and the marginal efficiency will decline; if the expenditures are complementary, expected revenues and the marginal efficiency will increase. Many government projects may have both effects. For example, the electricity program of the Tennessee Valley Authority lowered the marginal efficiency of capital for private utilities in the area but raised it for appliance dealers. Many other firms found a higher marginal efficiency of capital because their expected power costs declined. Most government activities are of this type, increasing the marginal efficiency for some firms and lowering it for others.

Even government transfer payments may affect the marginal efficiency of capital. Unemployment compensation payments tend to make workers less willing to accept low wages. Therefore, such payments raise labor costs and decrease the marginal efficiency of capital. (Nineteenth-century economists opposed the British Poor Laws along lines of reasoning similar to the above, thus helping to earn for economics its title of "the dismal science.")

The regulatory activities of the government also have their effect. Vigorous antitrust action will lower the marginal efficiency of capital for firms affected, since in fighting the case—even successfully—they might suffer a decrease in revenues or an increase in costs. Such action might, however, break down barriers to entry into the industry, thus raising the marginal efficiency for new firms. Protective tariffs raise the marginal efficiency for the protected firms, but lower it for firms which use the imported goods.

The general tenor of the administration may also have its effect on the marginal efficiency of capital. If businessmen feel that a certain administration is unfriendly to business, they may lower their estimates of future returns on the ground that the government will find some way to make the project unprofitable. If businessmen expect the government to go completely socialist in five years, they will have lower expectations of future revenues (zero for the sixth and succeeding years). As is so often the case with expectations, it does not matter whether these political predictions are correct or not, for unrealistic expectations decrease investment just as much as realistic ones.

The generally increased importance of government in the economic life of the nation is reflected by the increased attention paid to politics in business periodicals. As recently as 1932, *Business Week* made only occasional comments on the presidential elections. In recent elections, it provided detailed coverage of the campaign and the speeches of the candidates. Similar changes have been evident in the coverage by other business periodicals.

Supply *of* Funds

From the rather simplified discussion of investment, it seems that a firm need merely to make its determination of the marginal efficiency before it would borrow whatever funds it needed, provided that the market rate of interest was below the marginal efficiency. Unfortunately, most firms find the supply of funds more complicated.

The most important source of investment funds is not the market at all, but those funds generated internally by the firm. Corporations customarily retain a substantial portion of their earnings rather than paying them all out in dividends. (Most stockholders would rather have the funds invested by the firm, permitting earnings to be received and taxed as capital gains, not as income.) In addition, depreciation charges normally lead to accumulation of resources that can be used for investment. These internal funds are important to firms because the effective cost is very low. Investment outside the industry would lead the management outside its area of competence; investment in other firms within the industry might violate antitrust laws. These funds can also be used for purchases of bonds in the market, but their return might be as little as 3 percent. A firm can gain if it can make its own investments yield more than that. Most studies show close relationships between investment and these internal funds. (For this reason, profits become a doubly good indicator of investment: they are a clue to future profitability and also to present funds.)

When firms go to outside sources they often face a bewildering array of alternative sources. Large firms can sell securities on the stock exchanges or negotiate loans from insurance companies or other large lenders. Loans can be sought from banks or from individual investors. Finally, there is a variety of lenders providing discounts on receivables or other forms of funds. The range of interest rates is also very wide, varying from a rate near that on government bonds (for privately placed securities) to one near that on consumer small loans (for discounted receivables). The amounts that a given firm can borrow from each of these sources also vary according to the general credit-worthiness of the firm and the entire monetary situation.

In many cases, lenders do not change the nominal rate of interest, but become much more selective in their lending. These cases are often referred to as *capital rationing*. Since the nominal rate includes both a risk premium and the pure interest charge, more careful screening actually raises the pure interest by decreasing risk.

It is perhaps somewhat improper to call such a situation rationing. Most borrowers could still find funds, possibly from other lenders and often as higher cost. Nevertheless, there are often complaints, sometimes justified, that the choice of borrowers is made by lenders on the basis of goodwill, friendship, or even caprice. This discrimination has been one of the principal arguments for establishing government-lending programs, especially for agriculture and for small business.

These different sources of funds also cast some light on the question of response to changes in interest rates. Is the marginal-efficiency-of-capital schedule comparatively flat or steep? Various answers have been given to this question. For many years, economists had come to believe that little response was shown to changes in interest rates; however, some recent studies have indicated otherwise. The discussion above clearly indicates why some reaction should normally occur.

If a firm found itself unable to finance through its usual sources, it is often reluctant to shift to the next most expensive source or to sell its securities at a discount. (A discount is merely a device for converting the yield on a 6-percent bond at 8 percent.) This unwillingness to seek more expensive financing often means that substantial changes in investment will result from modest changes in interest rates.

Types *of* Investment

The U.S. Department of Commerce separates private domestic investment into three categories: residential construction, producers' plant and equipment, and net change in business inventories. Figure 7.4 indicates the course of investment and its components in recent years. Each of these components is subject to its own peculiarities and is worthy of brief comment.

Residential construction seems to depend mostly upon the growth of the society and the stock of old buildings. The demand for housing space is relatively stable, changing mainly with population and family structure. The stock of old houses is the result of the past building less the losses caused by wear and tear. Although one would expect such conditions to make residential construction a relatively stable component of investment, this has not been the case. The housing industry is characterized by a multitude of small contractors. The number grows in good times and falls off in poor times. The fragmentation of housing "manufacture" customarily results in over-building during housing booms; this overbuilding results in turn in depressed rents and selling prices and, consequently, in few new homes being built. During the lean years, many contractors drop out and many building-trades workmen shift to other industries. Gradually the depreciation of older homes and the growth of population create a condition of higher prices and higher rents. Since it takes time to reorganize the industry, the demand usually becomes acute before it is met. Then the process starts over again.

If the supply of, and the demand for, residential housing had originally been equal, they might have continued to be so. Boom construction tends to repeat itself, and the bunching in age distribution of houses will tend to mean a bunching of replacement needs. In the United States, the cycle from boom to boom customarily lasts about 17 years, although one might imagine a situation in which new construction methods (and a change in the durability of houses) could alter this time span.

Certain government activities have been undertaken to simplify the financing of home construction, notably under the Federal Housing Administration and, for veterans, under the so-called G.I. Bill of Rights. These programs involve government insurance of the loan so as to reduce the risk to the lender. These reductions of risk have effectively lowered the market rate of interest and made buyers eligible for mortgage credit. In this manner, they have greatly reduced

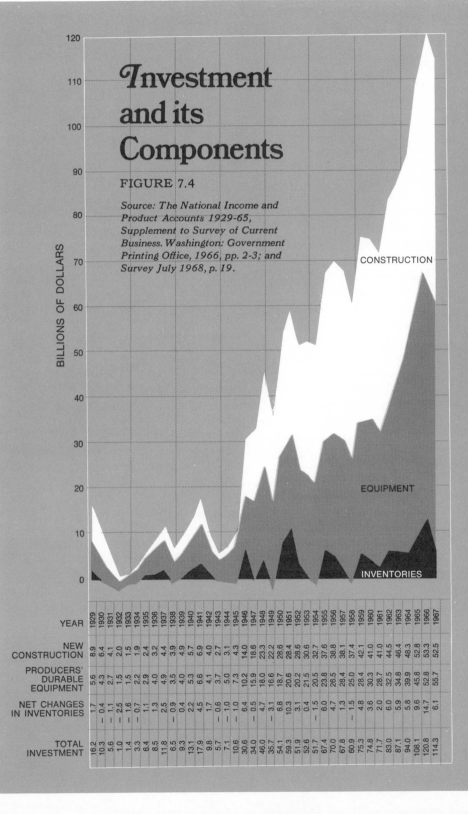

Investment and its Components

FIGURE 7.4

Source: The National Income and Product Accounts 1929-65, Supplement to Survey of Current Business. Washington: Government Printing Office, 1966, pp. 2-3; and Survey July 1968, p. 19.

BILLIONS OF DOLLARS

CONSTRUCTION

EQUIPMENT

INVENTORIES

YEAR	NEW CONSTRUCTION	PRODUCERS' DURABLE EQUIPMENT	NET CHANGES IN INVENTORIES	TOTAL INVESTMENT
1929	8.9	5.6	1.7	16.2
1930	6.4	4.3	– 0.4	10.3
1931	4.1	2.7	– 1.1	5.6
1932	2.0	1.5	– 2.5	1.0
1933	1.5	1.5	– 1.6	1.4
1934	1.9	2.2	0.7	3.3
1935	2.4	2.9	1.1	6.4
1936	3.2	4.0	1.3	8.5
1937	4.4	4.9	2.5	11.8
1938	3.9	3.5	– 0.9	6.5
1939	4.9	4.0	0.4	9.3
1940	5.7	5.3	2.2	13.1
1941	6.9	6.6	4.5	17.9
1942	4.0	4.1	1.7	9.8
1943	2.7	3.7	– 0.6	5.7
1944	3.1	5.0	– 1.0	7.1
1945	4.3	7.3	– 1.0	10.6
1946	14.0	10.2	6.4	30.6
1947	18.6	15.9	– 0.5	34.0
1948	23.3	18.0	4.7	46.0
1949	22.2	16.6	– 3.1	35.7
1950	28.6	18.7	6.8	54.1
1951	28.4	20.6	10.3	59.3
1952	28.6	20.2	3.1	51.9
1953	30.6	21.5	0.4	52.6
1954	32.7	20.5	– 1.5	51.7
1955	37.6	23.8	6.0	67.4
1956	38.8	26.5	4.7	70.0
1957	38.1	28.4	1.3	67.8
1958	37.4	25.0	– 1.5	60.9
1959	42.1	28.4	4.8	75.3
1960	41.0	30.3	3.6	74.8
1961	41.0	28.7	2.0	71.7
1962	44.5	32.5	6.0	83.0
1963	46.4	34.8	5.9	87.1
1964	48.3	39.9	5.8	94.0
1965	52.8	45.8	9.6	108.1
1966	53.3	52.8	14.7	120.8
1967	52.5	55.7	6.1	114.3

"capital rationing" in the construction field. Unfortunately, they have had the effect of making new construction very responsive to small changes in the interest rate. Since maximum interest rates for these loans are specified by law, a slight change in market rates may make lenders unwilling to make such loans. Thus guaranteed mortgage loans have responded violently to changes in interest rates.

If we include commercial construction in the consideration of durable equipment, we have plant and equipment for manufacturing, store and fixtures for retailing. These investments are more than all other investments combined and are closely related to the fluctuations of the national income which have come to be known as the "business cycle." They are subject to all the influences that have been discussed in this chapter.

Business inventories may change in either direction. In the analysis of these changes, the accelerator principle has perhaps its greatest usefulness. Most businesses prefer to maintain a fairly constant ratio between sales and inventories. Since these inventories can be sold off rather rapidly, there are seldom excess inventories for any long period of time. Because inventories are turned over within a relatively short period of time, no extended series of expected returns appears, but only the expected return when they are sold (soon). Thus all the conditions for the application of the accelerator are met. The relatively short turnover and relative changeability of inventories leads to a short inventory cycle, usually about 40 months.

A second factor which is very important, especially in the analysis of raw-materials inventories, is expected change in the price level. In previous chapters, however, we have not been considering changes in price levels. We therefore leave this topic for later treatment.

PROBLEMS AND DISCUSSION QUESTIONS

1. What factors induce a firm to undertake innovation? What are the difficulties in a pure profit calculation?

2. Many decisions on investment are made by hired managers who are interested in their own salaries and power rather than in the profits of stockholders. What effect can this difference in concern have upon investment?

3. What do you think are the prospects for stagnation of investment?

4. How would investment be affected by businesses having motivations other than profit?

5. Summarize the procedure that you would suggest a large corporation use in making its investment decisions.

SUGGESTED ADDITIONAL READINGS

An analysis of the techniques of decision making is presented by George Katona *in* "Psychological Analysis of Business Decisions and Expectations," *American Economic Review,* vol. 36 (1946); and by J. Meyer and E. Kuh, *The Investment Decision* (Cambridge, Mass.: Harvard University Press, 1957). The latter volume emphasizes especially the role of internal funds.

The role of innovations has been especially emphasized by Joseph A. Schumpeter in *The Theory of Economic Development* (Cambridge, Mass.: Harvard University Press, 1934). *See also* Oscar Lange, "A Note on Innovations," *Review of Economic Statistics,* vol. 25 (1943).

The leading proponent of the stagnation thesis in this country is Alvin M. Hansen. *See especially* his "Economic Progress and Declining Population Growth," *American Economic Review,* vol. 29 (1939), reprinted in *Readings in Business Cycle Theory* (Homewood, Ill.; Richard D. Irwin, Inc., 1944) and his view 13 years later in *Savings in the Modern Economy,* Heller, Boddy, and Nelson, eds. (Minneapolis: University of Minnesota Press, 1953), Chapter 4. Against this theory, *compare* the views of George Terborgh, *The Bogey of Economic Maturity* (Chicago: Machinery and Allied Products Institute, 1945) and David McCord Wright, in *Savings in the Modern Economy,* Chapter 13.

The accelerator principle was originally stated by J. M. Clark in "Business Acceleration and the Law of Demand," *Journal of Political Economy* (1917), reprinted in *Readings in Business Cycle Theory.* In a more sophisticated form it was developed by Lloyd Metzler's "The Nature and Stability of Inventory Cycles," *Review of Economics and Statistics,* vol. 32 (1941).

The interest elasticity of the investment function is discussed by W. H. White *in* "Interest Inelasticity of Investment Demand," *American Economic Review,* vol. 46 (1956) and Lorie Tarshis *in* "The Marginal Efficiency of Capital Function," *American Economic Review,* vol. 51 (1961). *See also* the comment and Tarshis' reply one year later in this review.

The appropriate treatment of risk is discussed by Jack Hirshleifer, "Risk, the Discount Rate, and Investment Decisions," *American Economic Review, Papers and Proceedings,* vol. 51 (1961).

Many aspects of investment are discussed in *Determinants of Investment Behavior,* Robert Ferber, ed. Proceedings of a conference of the University-National Bureau Committee for Economic Research, (New York: Columbia University Press, 1967). The articles by John Lintner and Dale W. Jorgensen are especially useful.

Part II of *The Brookings Quarterly Econometric Model of the United States,* edited by J. S. Duesenbery and others (Chicago: Rand McNally, 1965) discussed many problems in the estimation of investment behavior.

$\mathcal{A}$ppendix to Chapter 7

CALCULATION OF INVESTMENT YIELDS

The detailed calculation of yields is given in standard texts on mathematics of investment, but it will be worthwhile to summarize them here.

First, let us imagine a machine that costs $1000, lasts for only one year, and whose product can be sold at the end of the year for $1080 above out-of-pocket costs. For such a machine, the marginal efficiency of capital is 8 percent, for at that rate it would be possible to borrow the $1000, repay the principal ($1000) and the interest ($80) at the end of the year, and just break even. Such an investment would be profitable at any rate below 8 percent, unprofitable above it. If we call the present value Q and the return R, then

$$Q(1 + r) = R \qquad \text{(A7.1)}$$
$$\$1000(1.08) = \$1080 \qquad \text{(A7.2)}$$

Note that it was necessary to multiply by $(1 + r)$, since the borrower must repay the principal *and* the interest.

Similarly, knowing the return, we could find the present value by

$$Q = \frac{R}{1 + r} \qquad \text{(A7.3)}$$

$$\$1000 = \frac{\$1080}{1.08} \qquad \text{(A7.4)}$$

In a simple case like this it would be possible to solve directly for r. However, we might also do so by a simple process of trial and error. At 6 percent the present value of $1080 in one year is $1019 ($1080/1.06); at 8 percent, $1000 ($1080/1.08); and at 10 percent, $982 ($1080/1.10). Since the cost is $1000, the marginal efficiency of capital is 8 percent, for at that rate the present value equals the cost.

If this machine were to yield its $1080 only at the end of the second year, the marginal efficiency would be slightly less than 4 percent. If we borrowed money at 4 percent to buy the machine, we would owe $1040 ($1.04 \times \$1000$) at the end of the first year and $1081.60 ($1.04 \times \$1040$) at the end of the second year. Actually, the marginal efficiency would be 3.92 percent. The formula for such a computation would be

$$(1 + r)^2 Q = R \qquad (A7.5)$$
$$(1.0392)^2 \times \$1000 = \$1080 \qquad (A7.6)$$

or it could be stated as

$$Q = \frac{R}{(1 + r)^2} \qquad (A7.7)$$

If the return came at the end of three years the divisor would be $(1 + r)^3$; if it came at the end of four years, $(1 + r)^4$; and so on.

Most investments, in fact, do not yield a single return, but rather a return for each of many years, or even for each month or day. In such cases, the present value of the stream is the sum of the present values of each return in the stream. If $R_1, R_2 \ldots, R_n$ are the returns in each year; $Q_1, Q_2 \ldots, Q_n$ the present values of each of these returns; and Q the over-all present value, then

$$Q = Q_1 + Q_2 + \cdots + Q_n$$
$$= \frac{R_1}{1 + r} + \frac{R_2}{(1 + r)^2} + \cdots + \frac{R_n}{(1 + r)^n} \qquad (A7.8)$$

The marginal efficiency of capital is that value of r which makes the present value equal to the original purchase price. To find this value, insert the values of the returns ($R_1, R_2, \ldots R_n$) set Q equal to the purchase price, and solve for r. If the machine will last for more than two years, this solution is extremely difficult. It is usually easier to guess at a value for r, solve for Q, and compare the result with the cost. If Q is greater than the cost, the guess was too low.

We can then keep trying until we find the marginal efficiency of capital.

The problems at the end of this Appendix are designed to clarify the arithmetical process of determining the marginal efficiency of capital.

APPENDIX PROBLEMS

1. Company A is considering the purchase of a machine that costs $1000, will last for two years, and is expected to produce 500 units of output per year. These products sell at $4 and use raw materials costing $1.50 each. The machines will require 250 labor hours per year at $1.70 per hour. Selling cost for this product is estimated at $22 per month.

a. Find the net annual return for this machine. Do not deduct depreciation.
b. Assuming that all costs and revenues are concentrated at the end of each year, find the present value of the return if the interest rate is 6 percent.
c. Find the present value at 8 percent.
d. Find the present value at 10 percent.
e. What is the marginal efficiency for capital for this machine?

2. Other companies are considering the purchase of machines with the following costs and marginal efficiencies:

Company	Cost ($)	Marginal Efficiency (%)
B	10,000	7
C	7000	12
D	30,000	5
E	5000	15
F	22,000	10

Draw up the marginal-efficiency-of-capital schedule for these six companies (including A):

3. What amount of investment will take place if the market rate of interest is 9 percent? if the interest rate is 6 percent?

to some out ahead
country should have a
greater value of exports
than imports thus making
a profit

8

Foreign Trade

In Chapter 2 we noted that exports constitute a market for a significant portion of national product (about $46 billion in 1967). Against this, imports provide an alternative source of supply of goods that American consumers and businesses wish to buy ($41 billion in 1967). Although these amounts are small compared to domestic investment, consumption, and government spending, they are not negligible. It is therefore desirable to examine them, at least briefly.

In the simplest sense, it is appropriate to consider exports an exogenous variable, determined by conditions in other countries. It can therefore be treated as one of the injections into the system. Imports, on the other hand, are a leakage, since they are a part of income which is not automatically respent for domestic products. Like the other leakages, saving and taxes, imports are not exogenous, but depend upon the level of domestic income. As income rises, increasing our desire to buy goods and services, it also increases our desire to buy imported goods. Let us restate the equations of Chapter 5 with the changes to allow for exports and imports.

ADDITIONAL VARIABLES

Exogenous:

X = Exports

Endogenous:

M = Imports

net exports

EQUATIONS

$$Y = C + I + G + (X - M) \tag{8.1}$$

$$C = a + bY_D \tag{8.2}$$

$$Y_D = Y - Tx + Tr \tag{8.3}$$

$$I = I_0 \tag{8.4}$$

$$G = G_0 \tag{8.5}$$

$$Tx - Tr = T_0 + hY \tag{8.6}$$

$$X = X_0 \tag{8.7}$$

$$M = M_0 + mY \tag{8.8}$$

All the equations here are familiar, except for Equation 8.1, which has been changed to allow for net exports $(X - M)$, and Equations 8.7 and 8.8. Equation 8.7 merely specifies the exogenous character of exports, while Equation 8.8 gives a linear relationship between imports and income. (The coefficient m can be called the marginal propensity to import.) If all imports were consumer goods, it would be appropriate to relate imports to disposable income. Since many imports are used for investment, it seems appropriate to relate imports to total income.

As we did in Chapters 4 and 5, we combine all the other equations into Equation 8.1 and then solve for Y. We then obtain

$$Y = \frac{1}{1 - b + bh + m} (a - bT_0 + I_0 + G_0 + X_0 - M_0) \tag{8.9}$$

From this it follows that the investment, government spending, and export multipliers will be

$$k = \frac{1}{1 - b + bh + m} = \frac{1}{(1 - b)(1 - h) + h + m} \tag{8.10}$$

Foreign Trade and Equilibrium Income

FIGURE 8.1

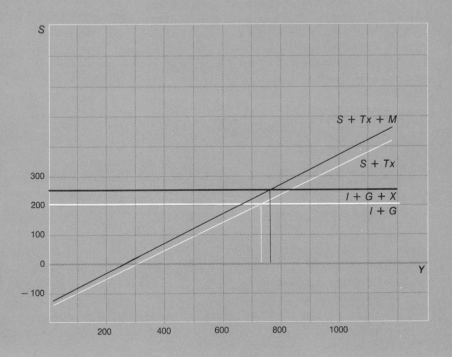

Thus the denominator of the multiplier represents the sum of the three leakage ratios: the effective marginal propensity to save, the marginal tax rate, and the marginal propensity to import. (Compare this multiplier with that given in Equation A5.20.) This multiplier is smaller than previous multipliers, since the denominator is larger.

By a similar process, one can alter the diagrams showing equilibrium income. We start with the basic diagram given in Figure 5.3, showing injections $(I + G)$ and leakages $(S + Tx)$. We now add exports to the injections and imports to the leakages. Since exports are exogenous, the new injection line is parallel to the old one. Imports are endogenous, and the new leakage line is not parallel to the old one. The results are shown in Figure 8.1.

The net balance of trade is the difference between exports and imports. One can observe this balance of trade in Figure 8.1 as the difference between exports and imports at the equilibrium income. This difference is the same as the difference between other leakages (excluding imports) and other injections (excluding exports). In Figure 8.1, the balance of trade is positive.

International economics commonly focuses on the balance of payments, not the balance of trade. This balance includes many capital flow and financial items in addition to the goods and services that represent the balance of trade. However, analysis of these factors would lead us afield from the concerns of this book. They are discussed in all standard texts in international economics.

Foreign Repercussions

For a small country that is a small part of world trade, the explanation of the last section is sufficient. For larger countries that account for more trade, some additional analysis is required. Let us imagine a simple two-country world, with each country having a multiplier of $2\frac{1}{2}$ and a marginal propensity to import of $\frac{1}{10}$. In country A, additional investment touches off a boom, leading to increased income of $10 billion. This increase will cause increased imports from B of $1 billion. The multiplier in B will increase incomes there by $2.5 billion. Country B in turn will increase its imports from A by $250 million. Thus the exports of country A are not wholly exogenous,

Foreign Trade
with Repercussions

FIGURE 8.2

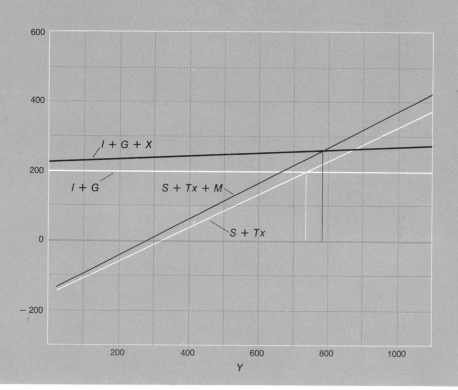

but increase with every increase in income of country A, operating through the repercussions on country B. The corresponding equilibrium diagram is shown in Figure 8.2, in which the injection line including exports contains a slight slope.

Our example probably represents an extreme case of the foreign repercussions. In most cases the effects would be much less. Even if the marginal propensity to import were as large as $\frac{1}{10}$, the effect would be dissipated among various countries, with only a portion of the increase coming back to the country that initiated the expansion. It is true that there would be second and third round effects, as A increases its exports to C, which has benefited from the increased exports to B; but the total effects are apt to be quite small nevertheless. It would be very surprising if any country had a marginal propensity to export as high as 1 percent.

In this chapter we have been discussing the role of foreign trade in aggregate analysis. In future chapters, in order to simplify the presentation, we shall ignore foreign effects. Those who wish may put them in everywhere, adding exports to the injections and imports to the leakages.

SUGGESTED ADDITIONAL READINGS

The graphic treatment of this chapter is adapted from C. P. Kindleberger, *International Economics*, 3d ed. (Homewood, Ill.: Richard D. Irwin, Inc., 1963) Chapter 10.

For an algebraic treatment, *see* Ingo Walter, *International Economics—Theory and Policy* (New York: Ronald Press, 1968) Chapter 13.

9

The Commodity Market

The determination of income was discussed in Chapters 4 and 5, using increasingly complex models. There it was seen that a specific income level corresponds to each level of investment and that changes in income are related by the multiplier to changes in investment. In Chapter 7, we saw that the marginal-efficiency-of-capital schedule relates investment to the rate of interest. By applying the multiplier to this schedule, we can derive the income response to every change in the rate of interest. We shall not calculate an interest multiplier, partly because this would require exact knowledge of the shape of the marginal-efficiency schedule and partly because it would not provide the proper tools for future discussions. Instead, we shall see how all the relationships previously discussed can be combined into a single relationship, giving income as a function of the rate of interest.

In the next chapter we shall investigate the money market to see what factors determine the rate of interest. At the moment, we shall content ourselves with deriving a *schedule* giving the relationship between income and the rate of interest. (This is analogous to deriving a supply curve or a demand curve. The work here will not determine either the rate of interest or the level of income, just as a demand curve alone will not determine the price or quantity.) We shall use the system of Chapter 5, with the addition of the marginal-efficiency-of-capital schedule:

VARIABLES

Endogenous:

Y = Income
C = Consumption
I = Investment
S = Saving
Y_D = Disposable income

Exogenous:

G = Government expenditures
Tx = Taxes
Tr = Transfers
r = Rate of interest

EQUATIONS

$$Y = C + I + G \tag{9.1}$$
$$C = a + bY_D \tag{9.2}$$
$$Y_D = Y - Tx + Tr \tag{9.3}$$
$$I = f(r) \tag{9.4}$$
$$G = G_0 \tag{9.5}$$
$$Tx = Tx_0 \tag{9.6}$$
$$Tr = Tr_0 \tag{9.7}$$
$$S = Y_D - C \tag{9.8}$$

It should be noted that there are eight equations, but nine unknowns. This is therefore an open system, which can be closed only by giving an explanation of the rate of interest. However, this system can be simplified by reducing it to one equation with two unknowns, r and Y. The system will still be open but will be simpler.

In order to find the relationship between income and the rate of interest, we can start with a rate of interest chosen at random. From

Equation 9.4, the marginal efficiency of capital, we can find the corresponding investment. This investment and the level of government spending can be added to calculate the total level of injections into the system. The saving function and taxes and transfers can be combined to find the level of leakages appropriate to each level of income. The income appropriate to the initial rate of interest is the one for which the level of leakages equals the level of injections. By repeating this process for other rates of interest, a complete schedule can be derived relating income and interest.

Given the behavior of the government, each of the points on this schedule represents a combination of the rate of interest and the level of income that would result from the adjustment of consumers and investors. Since this adjustment consists of variation in the purchase of goods and services, such actions are said to take place in the commodity market. For each rate of interest, there is one level of income that represents *equilibrium*—that is, a level from which there is no tendency to depart, either through the actions of consumers or through the actions of investors. Because each point represents such an equilibrium as far as purchases of goods and services are concerned, such a function is referred to as the *commodity equilibrium curve*. Historically, however, economists have given it the name *IS curve*, thus representing the combination of interest and income where planned saving would equal planned investment. Although this analysis includes other factors, such as government spending, this traditional name will be retained.

The process of actually deriving the *IS* curve can be simplified by following the model of Chapter 5, using the saving function. Combining the definition of saving (Equation 9.8) with the definitions of disposable income (Equation 9.3) and income (Equation 9.1), we obtain

$$
\begin{aligned}
S &= Y_D - C \\
&= Y - Tx + Tr - C \\
&= C + I + G - Tx + Tr - C \\
&= I + G - (Tx - Tr)
\end{aligned}
\tag{9.9}
$$

Adding $Tx - Tr$ to both sides, we obtain the equilibrium condition

$$
S + Tx - Tr = I + G \tag{9.10}
$$

In other words, total leakages equal total injections.

We can now derive the *IS* curve using this equilbirium condition. Choose a rate of interest at random and find the appropriate level of investment from the marginal-efficiency-of-capital schedule. Adding government spending to this investment to find total injections, we find total leakages from the equilibrium condition. Then we use the saving function, adjusted for the level of taxes and transfers, to find the income level that corresponds to these leakages. Repeating this process for other interest rates, we derive the entire *IS* curve.

This process can be used in a numerical fashion. The subparts of Table 9.1 show the schedules that correspond to each of the equations given.

Assume a rate of interest of 20 percent. From the marginal efficiency of capital (Part A), we find that the resulting rate of investment

TABLE 9.1

DERIVATION OF A HYPOTHETICAL *IS* CURVE
(UNIT: $1 BILLION)

PART A		PART B		PART C	
Marginal Efficiency of Capital		Equilibrium Saving[a]		Saving Function[b]	
r	I	I	$S + (Tx - Tr)$	Y	$S + (Tx - Tr)$
20	30	10	140	600	140
15	70	30	160	650	160
10	110	50	180	700	180
5	150	70	200	750	200
		90	220	800	220
		110	240	850	240
		130	260	900	260
		150	280	950	280
				1000	300

[a] Assuming government spending of $130 billion.
[b] This is the saving function of Table 5.4, assuming $Tx - Tr$ of 100.

TABLE 9.2

HYPOTHETICAL *IS* CURVE
(UNIT: $1 BILLION)

r (%)	Y
20	650
15	750
10	
5	950

is $30 billion. Using this investment and assuming government expenditures of $130 billion, we find (Part B) total injections and leakages of $160 billion. From the saving function (Part C) we find that this will result from an income level of $650 billion. This gives us one point on the *IS* curve. Similarly, we find an income of $750 billion corresponding to 15 percent and an income of $950 billion corresponding to 5 percent. We list these values in Table 9.2. The student should fill in the income corresponding to the rate of 10 percent.

It should be noted that Part *A* of Table 9.1 is derived from Figure 7.1 and Part *C*, from the data of Table 5.4.

The same process can be performed graphically. Figure 9.1 corresponds exactly to Table 9.1. The process also corresponds.

Part (A): Choose a rate of interest at random—say, 20 percent. From the marginal-efficiency-of-capital schedule we find the corresponding level of investment, $30 billion. Part (A) is merely Figure 7.1.

Part (B): To find the equilibrium level of saving, add to the $30 billion of investment the $130 billion of government expenditure. To do this, draw a 45° line upward starting from $130 billion, the assumed G_0. Thus, when I equals zero, $S + Tx - Tr$ equals 130; for every dollar of increase in investment, saving also increases by one dollar. In this particular case, a saving of $160 billion corresponds to an investment of $30 billion.

Part (C): From the saving function is found the level of income ($650 billion) which corresponds to the saving level of $160 billion. Part (C) is the same as Figure 5.2.

Equilibrium of the Commodity Market

FIGURE 9.1

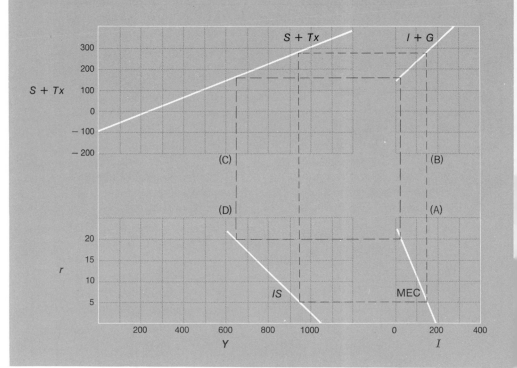

Part (D): Plot this income ($650 billion) against the 20-percent rate of interest with which we started.

Repeating the process for other rates of interest gives other income values. When these are all plotted in Part (D), they can be connected to produce the *IS* curve; Part (D) corresponds to Table 9.2.

The parts of Figure 9.1 have been drawn so that the scales run exactly the same. In this way, a line drawn parallel to one of the axes will cut two graphs at the same value. The line drawn upward from $30 billion investment in Part (A) hits Part (B) at $30 billion investment; the line drawn across from Part (B) at $160 billion leakage hits Part (C) at $160 billion. The construction of Part (D) then consists of finding the fourth corner of the rectangle whose base is drawn at 20-percent interest and whose corners are the graphs of Parts (A), (B), and (C). A new rectangle is drawn at 5 percent, and finally enough points are available to construct the graph of Part (D).

This *IS* curve then is merely a summary of the functions that were previously discussed. Therefore, any change in any of the basic functions will cause a change in the *IS* curve. The student should prove for himself that an increase in government expenditures, an increase in the marginal efficiency of capital, or a decrease in the saving function will move the *IS* curve to the right; that opposite shifts will move it to the left. The multipliers presented in Chapter 5 give the ratio between changes in government activities and the horizontal movement of the *IS* curve. The investment multiplier gives the ratio between a horizontal shift of the marginal efficiency of capital and the horizontal shift of the *IS* curve.

Nothing can be said about the equilibrium level of income until something is known about the rate of interest. To understand the level of the rate of interest, it is necessary to examine the structure of the money market. Some people will believe that such study is unnecessary since the government is a very important part of the money market. Such people summarize the money market thus: The government chooses a rate of interest, then does whatever is necessary to produce that rate of interest. If this were true, the following equation could be added

$$r = r_0 \tag{9.11}$$

indicating that the rate of interest is an exogenous variable determined by the government for its own reasons. Then it could be said that economics can be divided into two parts: real economics, dealing with goods and services produced at a fixed interest rate; and mone-

tary theory, which teaches Treasury and Federal Reserve Board officials how to fix the interest rate. This view might be partly justified,
but it is preferable to examine the money market and see exactly
what is involved in setting the interest rate. Only in this way can
we understand the relations between fiscal policy and monetary policy.
Those who prefer to omit such study may insert Equation 9.11, representing it by a horizontal line on Part (D) of Figure 9.1. For those
who prefer some such understanding, Chapter 10 briefly reviews the
workings of the money market.

PROBLEMS AND DISCUSSION QUESTIONS

1. Assume that $C = 50 + \frac{3}{4}Y_D$, $G = 100$, $Tx = 90$ and
$Tr = 10$.
The marginal efficiency of capital is as follows:

r	I
20	40
15	80
10	120
5	160

Draw up the IS curve.
2. From the information given in Problem 1, show the
graphic derivation of the IS curve. (Use Figure 9.1 as
a model.)
3. What would be the IS curve if G were 60 instead
of 100?

SUGGESTED ADDITIONAL READINGS

The basic concepts of the commodity market and money
market are adapted from J. R. Hicks in "Mr. Keynes
and the Classics," *Econometrica* (April 1937), reprinted
in *Readings in the Theory of Income Distribution* (Homewood, Ill.: Richard D. Irwin, Inc., 1946).

cAppendix to Chapter 9

The text of this chapter indicates the difficulty of deriving an *IS* curve algebraically because of the generalized shape of the marginal efficiency of capital. However, if one assumes that this relation is linear (as the graphs and numerical tables do), an algebraic solution is easily derived. Let us use the equation system from the beginning of the chapter, with a linear marginal efficiency of capital (Equation A9.3).

$$Y = C + I + G \qquad (9.1)$$
$$C = a + bY_D \qquad (9.2)$$
$$Y_D = Y - Tx + Tr \qquad (9.3)$$
$$I = I_0 - dr \qquad (A9.1)$$
$$G = G_0 \qquad (9.5)$$
$$Tx = Tx_0 \qquad (9.6)$$
$$Tr = Tr_0 \qquad (9.7)$$

By substituting Equations 9.2, A9.1, and 9.5 into Equation 9.1 and then applying the definition of Y_D from Equation 9.3, we obtain

$$Y = C + I + G$$
$$= a + bY_D + I_0 - dr + G_0$$
$$= a + b(Y - Tx_0 + Tr_0) + I_0 - dr + G_0$$
$$= a + bY - bTx_0 + bTr_0 + I_0 - dr + G_0$$

$$(A9.2)$$

Simplifying, we obtain

$$Y - bY = a - bTx_0 + bTr_0 + I_0 + G_0 - dr \quad (A9.3)$$

$$Y = \frac{1}{1-b}(a - bTx_0 + bTr_0 + I_0 + G_0)$$

$$-\frac{d}{1-b}r \quad (A9.4)$$

We note that this equation for the IS curve can be divided into two parts: the first gives the level of Y when r is zero; the second shows the change in Y for each change in r. This latter term is composed of the multiplier and the slope of the marginal-efficiency-of-capital schedule.

10

The Money Market

Interest is the price paid by the borrower to the lender of money. Therefore, our discussions of the money market are also discussions of the rate of interest, for anything that affects borrowing and lending will affect the interest rate. Interest has already come to our attention in preceding chapters because it has an important effect upon the level of investment. Now we must consider the factors that determine the rate of interest.

In this chapter, we shall assume, for the purposes of the discussion, that there is such a thing as _the_ rate of interest. As a matter of fact, there is a range of rates of interest and an even wider variation in _apparent_ rates of interest. Government bonds carry interest rates as low as 3 percent and as high as 5 percent. State and municipal bonds carry lower interest rates because they are tax exempt; corporation bonds, higher rates. If you wish to borrow money to buy a house, the interest rate is 6 to 7½ percent; to buy a new automobile, 10 to 14 percent; and a personal loan from a small-loan company carries a charge of 3 percent per month—a total of 36 percent per year.

What causes these variations? In large part, they are the result of other costs which are often stated as part of the rate of interest but which are actually payments for something other than the mere lending of money. Foremost among these other costs is the risk premium. A man might be willing to give up the use of his money for a year for 6 percent if he is certain to get the money back. However, if there is a chance that the money may not be returned, he will demand a higher payment to compensate him for his risk. If the lender has found that for every 20 borrowers who repay there is one who does not, he will charge each of the 20 an extra 5 percent to recover the loss incurred on the loan that is *not* repaid. Naturally, the less risky the loans, the lower will be the premium. This is why the federal government can borrow money at a very low rate of interest, for the risk premium is negligible. This risk premium also accounts for many of the variations in rates paid by states and municipalities.

Many loans involve large amounts of clerical expense. For this reason, any small loan will carry a very high "interest rate" merely to cover the administrative costs. At the small-loan rate—36 percent per year—the charge on a one-month loan of $25 would be 75¢. Even at this rate, the company probably loses money on such a loan, for the 75-cent charge must cover the cost of checking credit references, recording the loan, and accepting and recording the repayment. Any firm that makes a loan as small as $25 therefore usually does so only for advertising purposes.

After all these other charges are subtracted from the apparent interest rate, there still remain substantial variations in the "pure" rate of interest. Such variations usually depend upon the period of the loan and are related to opportunities which may be foregone by holding the loan. A person who lends money for three months knows that he will have the principal and interest back at the end of that period of time. If new opportunities should develop within that period, he will soon have funds to take advantage of them. Since such a loan is almost the same as cash, it carries an interest rate almost the same as cash—that is, near zero. (In the United States during World War II, one could earn less than two dollars by lending the government a thousand dollars for three months.) The longer the loan commitment, the greater the chance of passing up a good opportunity. If you lend money for 20 years at, say, 4 percent, it is quite possible that at some time during the 20 years you will have an opportunity to invest the money at 6 percent. For this reason, lenders demand, and receive, higher payments on long-term securities to compensate for the possible alternatives that have been foregone. Thus, even the "pure" rate of interest may vary from, say, 3 to 5 percent, depending upon the duration of the loan.

Our primary concern with the rate of interest is its effect on investment. Since investments are usually made for relatively long periods, we are most interested in the long-term rate of interest and we shall speak as though it were the only one. It probably makes little difference which rate we discuss, for long- and short-term rates tend to fluctuate at the same time and to about the same degree. Any movement in the long-term rate is usually matched by a corresponding movement in shorter-term rates. Because the rates are so interrelated, the factors that explain one (the long-term rate) explain all of them.

Transactions Demand for Money

Since the interest rate is the price of money, we must consider now the supply and demand for money. The term *supply and demand for money* is apt to be confusing, so it will pay us to pause a moment for definitions. What we mean by *money* is a certain *stock* of funds rather than a *flow* of spending power. In common usage, we speak of desire for money to pay our current bills, for the landlord, the grocer, the gas station. This is a desire for income. One might imagine paying all these bills without ever having any stock of money. If all purchases were made on credit and paid for by check simultaneously with depositing a pay check, all the things for which we say we want money would be supplied without our having any money balance more than temporarily. By a demand for money, we are referring to a desire to have an average balance in the checking account of, say, $500, or to be able to carry $50 in our pocket. In accordance with common usage, we will define money to include currency, coins, and bank deposits.

Elementary textbooks point out that money is a medium of exchange and a store of value. These two uses constitute the demand for money. For the sake of simplicity, we shall temporarily assume that the two uses are independent so that we can discuss them separately.

As a medium of exchange, money is needed to finance transactions. If, as we imagined above, we made all purchases on credit and paid for them by check, no money would be needed. If the whole society operated in the same way, all transactions could be financed by an elaborate juggling of credits the first of every month. Because our entire society does not operate in this fashion, some average stock of money is needed to finance the time intervals between receipt of income and its expenditure on consumption. Similarly, firms need some stock of money to pay bills for goods that are purchased and later sold. The more transactions there are in a society, the greater the stock of money required for these time intervals. The greater the use of credit, the less money is required. If consumption spending were distributed uniformly and if income were received once a month, the stock of money required by a consumer would range from 30 days' consumption (at the beginning of the month) down to zero (at the end), averaging a half month's expenses. If many items are paid for at the beginning of the month, the required stock for the remainder of the period will be less. If all business were in control of a single large corporation, little money would be needed for interfirm transactions; if all firms were very small, much would be needed.

In Chapter 3, this demand for money was discussed using the term "velocity" for the ratio between the amount of money required and the level of income. If the transactions demand is represented as M_1, we can state this demand as

$$M_1 = T(Y) \tag{10.1}$$

Here again we have used a general function, to be read M_1 equals T of Y. This, we could restate in terms of the equation of exchange

$$M_1 V_1 = Y \tag{10.2}$$

$$M_1 = \frac{Y}{V_1} \tag{10.3}$$

In the last section of this chapter, however, other factors that might affect this demand will be discussed; so, it will be better to use the general form. In any case, it is clear that such a function is upward sloping. For the same reasons of simplicity that a linear consumption function was used, a linear transactions demand will be used, thereby assuming a constant velocity. Figure 10.1 gives a possible shape for this function. Since this demand is for currency and bank balances for day-to-day use, it is sometimes referred to as a demand for *active* balances.

Sometimes money is held for *precautionary* purposes: not to be used for expected transactions, but only to be available in case of emergency. It seems reasonable, however, to include this precautionary demand with ordinary transactions, since both probably move together as a function of income.

Hypothetical Transactions Demand for Money

FIGURE 10.1

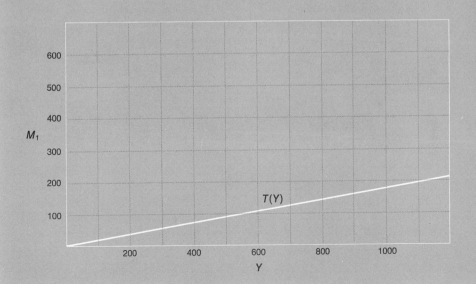

Liquidity Preference

The second aspect of the demand for money is as a store of value, that is, a demand for more passive balances. Such a demand was not included in the classical system because the classical economists did not see why anyone would wish to use money for this purpose when he could hold assets that earn an income. The analysis of passive balances is one of the major innovations of the Keynesian system.

When a person buys assets, such as bonds or other securities, he gives up control of his money for a time. In so doing, he renders himself unable to take advantage of future opportunities and becomes more vulnerable to future adversity. He can, of course, sell these assets in an attempt to regain his money, but he cannot always sell them at par value. If the current interest rate is 5 percent, no one would be willing to buy a 4-percent bond at par. The longer the period of time the old bond has left to run at the lower rate, the greater the discount if it is sold. The potential capital loss is a deterrent to any purchaser of securities. Any investor who expects the interest rate to rise will hold his cash rather than risk paying a premium to recover control of his funds.

The strength of this preference for liquidity varies from time to time, especially as interest rates change. When rates are low, one would expect that any changes would be upward. Thus, an investor would be foolish to risk a capital loss for a relatively small current return. At such a time, many investors prefer cash and few prefer securities. When interest rates are high, the opposite is true. One would expect only downward movements of rates, causing capital gains. Since current returns are also high in this case, most investors will forego liquidity and exchange cash for securities. Therefore, the demand for money as a store of value varies inversely with the rate of interest: the higher the rate of interest, the lower the demand for money; the lower the rate of interest, the higher the demand for money. Since this second demand for money depends upon the desire for liquidity, it is called the *liquidity-preference function* and is stated

$$M_2 = L(r) \tag{10.4}$$

Again, merely a general function, without specification as to its shape, has been presented. However, reasons for believing that it will slope downward have already been presented. The same kind of reasoning leads one to believe that at a low rate of interest security buyers would hold any amount of cash rather than bid for securities. At this interest rate, the demand for money becomes perfectly elastic, since the risk of capital loss from an increase in the interest rate is high and the return is negligible. Similarly, at high interest rates the demand for money would become completely inelastic, since the risk of capital loss would be slight and the return would be adequate compensation for such risk. Between these ranges, a linear function has again been used, as shown in Figure 10.2, although a moderate curvature might be more realistic.

Later in this chapter, we will assume that the interest rate is affected by the amount of M_2 which is available. By what process does this interest-rate adjustment come about? Let us assume a sudden increase in the money supply over and above that needed for ordinary transactions. If investors were previously satisfied with the proportion of cash to securities, they will not wish to hold this additional sum of cash and will try to buy securities. The increased demand for securities will tend to drive up the price of securities, since the present holders will also prefer the securities to cash. This process of price rises will continue until some security-holders are willing to accept the new cash rather than keep the securities. Since the price on old securities moves inversely with the rate of interest, a rise in the price of securities is equivalent to a decrease in the interest rate. Only when the interest rate is already at the minimum will buyers prefer to hold the new money rather than offer any premiums for securities.

Conversely, if there is a decrease in the amount of money available for passive balances, the security-holders will try to replenish their cash supplies. To do so they will sell securities. Since such securities will find buyers only at a discount, the price will fall, thus increasing the rate of interest.

By the process outlined above, the prices of securities and interest rates will seesaw until someone is willing to hold the available stock of money. If there is too much money for which holders must be found at the going rate of interest, a game of "hot potato" ensues, with each participant trying to get rid of the excess money and acquire securities. This process continues until the interest rate is forced down enough to balance the demands for money and for securities. If there is too little money, all investors scramble for it until interest rates are driven up. All money will always be held, but only after interest rates have adjusted along the liquidity-preference curve will everyone be satisfied.

Hypothetical Liquidity Preference Curve

FIGURE 10.2

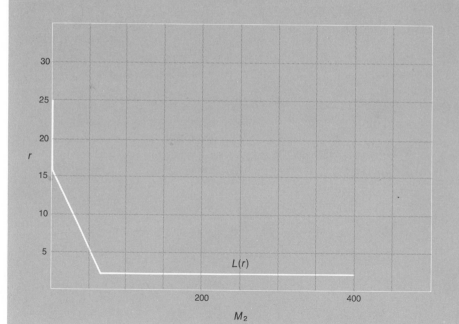

The Supply *of* Money

Liquidity preference and transactions demand together constitute the demand for money. Equilibrium in the money market can come about only when this demand is equal to the available supply.

To discuss all the attributes of the money supply would require a complete analysis of the banking system. Such an analysis would take us far afield, into a general discussion of central banking and deposit creation by the banking system. These discussions are part of any course or textbook in money and banking. For our purpose, it is sufficient to state that the money supply may be taken as an exogenous variable, substantially under the control of the Treasury and the Federal Reserve System. We indicate the exogenous nature of the money supply by

$$M_S = M_0 \tag{10.5}$$

Further discussion of the working of Federal Reserve policy is contained in the Appendix.

The LM Curve

The essential condition for equilibrium in the money market is that the supply of money equal the demand for money. This can be stated

$$M_S = M_1 + M_2 \tag{10.6}$$

With this condition, we are prepared to draw up the combinations of the rate of interest and the level of income which are consistent with equilibrium in the money market. The process is analogous to the derivation of the commodity equilibrium curve.

First we choose a level of income at random. From the transactions-demand function (Equation 10.1) we know how much money (M_1) will be needed to finance this income. Since the supply of money is fixed at a level M_0 by Equation 10.3, we can find the amount of money for passive balances by subtraction, since

$$M_1 + M_2 = M_S = M_0 \tag{10.7}$$

When we have found such an amount of M_2, then the liquidity-preference function will tell us the resulting rate of interest. This rate of interest can be plotted against the original income level. By repeating the process we derive other points. When we connect these points, we have a *money market equilibrium curve*—that is, the curve of all combinations of the rate of interest and the level of income that are consistent with equilibrium in the money market. Because this equilibrium depends upon the liquidity function and the money supply, it is called the *LM curve*.

Table 10.1 presents hypothetical data from which an *LM* curve

TABLE 10.1

DERIVATION OF A HYPOTHETICAL *LM* CURVE
(UNIT: $1 BILLION)

PART A		PART B		PART C	
Transactions Demand for Money		Money Demand Equals Money Supply[a]		Liquidity Preference	
Y	M_1	M_1	M_2	r	M_2
100	18	0	180	16	0
200	36	18	162	14	9
300	54	36	144	12	18
400	72	54	126	10	27
500	90	72	108	8	36
600	108	90	90	6	45
700	126	108	72	4	54
800	144	126	54	2	63 or more
900	162	144	36		
1000	180	162	18		
		180	0		

[a] Assuming M_S = $180 billion.

can be computed. Part A, the transactions demand for money, corresponds to Figure 10.1. Part C, the liquidity-preference function, corresponds to Figure 10.2. Part B merely expresses the equilibrium condition that the sum of the two demands must equal the money supply, in this case assumed to be $180 billion. Other combinations could be added to any column.

Let us choose an income at random—say $900 billion. From the transactions demand, Part A, we find that this level will require $162 billion of active balances. From Part B we see that this will leave $18 billion for idle holding. We can then expect, using the liquidity preference, Part C, that competition for this sum will drive the interest rate to 12 percent. This is one point on the *LM* curve.

Starting with a second income of $600 billion, we find a required M_1 of $108 billion. From Part B we find that $72 billion will be available for passive balances. From Part C we find that this amount will push the interest rate to 2 percent.

If we start with a $500-billion income, we find a required M_1 of $90 billion, leaving $90 billion available for M_2. However, since the minimal interest rate of 2 percent has been reached, the interest rate will not go below this level.

These values, along with others, have been plotted in Table 10.2.

TABLE 10.2

HYPOTHETICAL *LM* CURVE
(UNIT: $1 BILLION)

Y	r (%)
100	2
600	2
650	2
700	4
750	6
800	8
850	10
900	12
950	14
1000	16

Equilibrium of the Money Market

FIGURE 10.3

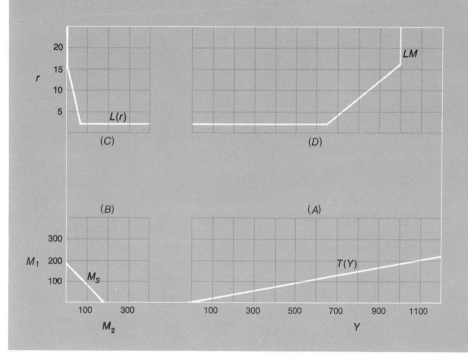

Most of the lower values have been omitted. Values of r accompanying incomes like $650 billion and $750 billion were obtained by interpolation on Parts A and B.

The same kind of analysis can be shown in graphic form. Figure 10.3 applies the information given in Table 10.1 to the development of an LM curve. Choose an income at random—say, $800 billion. In Part (A), it is seen that this will require $144 billion for transactions purposes. Part (B) is a 45° line downward, drawn so that the sum of M_1 and M_2 at every point is $180 billion. From Part (B), we find that liquidity preference will force an interest rate of 8 percent. This interest rate is plotted in Part (D) against the $800 billion income with which we started. By repeating this process for other incomes, other points on the LM curve are derived. Again the LM curve is obtained by finding the fourth corner of each of the rectangles drawn with corners on the three graphs representing transactions demand, money supply, and liquidity preference. The similarity of this derivation to that of the IS curve of Chapter 9 is clear.

Empirical Analysis

As we would expect, economists have devoted considerable attention to the analysis of money markets in order to understand better all of the factors that influence them. In particular, the liquidity-preference function, which plays such a special role in these markets, has been the object of special study.

One special problem is the existence of the *liquidity trap,* the horizontal portion of the liquidity-preference function. If this trap exists, there is an important limitation on the ability of the system to adjust, since downward movement of the interest rate is limited. Naturally, therefore, a large amount of statistical study has been designed, to test whether such a flat portion exists or whether the curve shows a relatively continuous downward slope. Different results have been obtained by different methods, but a majority of them seem to indicate such a trap. One example is shown in Figure 10.4.

There are also other factors besides the rate of interest which affect the demand for money. (Since these exogenous factors are not explicitly mentioned in the liquidity functions, they account for *shifts* in

The Statistical Liquidity Preference Function

FIGURE 10.4

Source: John H. Wood, Aggregate Liquidity Preference
Functions for the United States, 1919-1960, Purdue
University Institute for Quantitative Research in
Economics and Management, Institute Paper
Nov. 16, 1961.

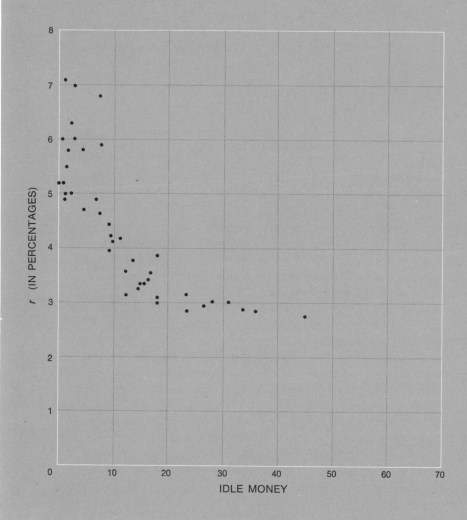

the function.) The most important of these seems to be the general wealth of the community. If one's holdings of stocks, bonds, and real assets grew, it is probable that one would want to hold a larger absolute amount in cash as well. The speculative demand for money depends primarily on a desire for maneuverability; the size of maneuverable wealth would certainly seem to depend upon general wealth. Such a prediction is borne out by statistical studies, which indicate a general shift of the liquidity function to the right as total wealth increases.

A closely related question is whether the transactions demand for money depends upon the interest rate. If the price of money were rather high, firms would be expected to try to economize on their use of cash. They might try to buy securities even for short periods, and, perhaps, make other purchases more frequently but in smaller amounts. Whether it would be worthwhile to do so would depend upon a balancing of the costs of keeping money for transactions and the extra administrative costs of making more but smaller transactions. It is probable, therefore, that the transactions demand shows very little reaction to interest rates except at rather high levels. Such a response would mean that the LM curve would always have some elasticity, instead of becoming strictly vertical as it does in Figure 10.3. However, the effect would be apparent only at improbably high interest rates, so that it would have little practical significance.

The discussion of the last two paragraphs indicates that the division between M_1 and M_2, between active and passive balances is a vague one, adopted for clarity in discussion. It is probably better to speak of the varied motives for holding money, including those which depend on income and those which depend on interest rates. Certainly, there are no observable magnitudes that correspond to M_1 and M_2. The statistical studies of liquidity preference (such as shown in Figure 10.4) require estimating an M_1, usually based on velocity, and subtracting from the total money supply to find M_2. An alternative is simply to combine Equations 10.1 and 10.4 into a general demand for money.

$$M_d = T(Y) + L(r) \tag{10.8}$$

It has also been questioned whether transactions velocity is constant at various income levels. One possibility is that as real income rises the total number of transactions also rises. However, this large number of separate transactions means that the fluctuations will be a smaller percentage of the average level. If transactions demand includes an amount to cover transactions plus an amount to cover the possible fluctuations, it is possible that this latter portion would grow less than proportionately. (The similarity to insurance is obvious.) In such a case, velocity would be slightly higher at higher incomes, thus imparting a downward curvature to the transactions-demand function.

A matter of even greater concern is whether the existence of substitutes for money drastically alters the demand for money. If one can hold savings-and-loan shares while waiting for speculative opportunities, use charge accounts for ordinary transactions, and use credit cards for precaution against emergencies, the demand for money itself is apt to be much less than before. (Checking accounts, which were once considered money substitutes, became such a good substitute we now consider them money.) As substitutes gain in importance the more likely it is that changes in the money supply may be offset by counteracting changes elsewhere. In such a case, we have not a demand for *money*, but a demand for *general liquidity*, of which money is only a small part. We would then face a dilemma. If we continue to calculate the *LM* curve on the basis of the demand and supply of money alone, it will be subject to violent shifts as changes in the money substitutes occur. If, on the other hand, we try to draw the *LM* curve in terms of general liquidity, then the supply can no longer be treated as an exogenous variable. An elaborate set of financial explanations would be required to link actions of the Federal Reserve System to the actual supply of *general liquidity*. Some hints at this approach are given in the Appendix, but no definite answers are possible yet. Indeed, such study is one of the most interesting areas of research into money-market phenomena.

PROBLEMS AND DISCUSSION QUESTIONS

1. What effect would increased use of charge accounts have on the transactions demand for money? Can you suggest other factors that would shift the transactions demand?

2. If investors became generally more optimistic about the future, would the liquidity-preference curve rise or fall? What other factors might cause changes in the curve?

3. The society requires, for transactions purposes, three months' income. The money supply is $300 billion and the liquidity preference is as follows:

r	M_2
15	30
10	90
5	150 or more

From these data, draw up the *LM* curve.

4. Using the data of Problem 3, show the graphic derivation of the *LM* curve.

5. How would an increase in the money supply to $400 billion affect the *LM* curve of Problem 3?

SUGGESTED ADDITIONAL READINGS

Keynes discussed the demand for money in *The General Theory of Employment, Interest, and Money*, Chapter 13. The idea that transactions demand may be interest-elastic derives principally from Alvin Hansen, *Monetary Theory and Fiscal Policy* (New York: McGraw-Hill, 1949), pp. 55–70.

Discussions of liquidity preference are plentiful. *See especially* John H. Wood, *Aggregate Liquidity Preference Functions for the United States, 1919–1960*, Purdue University Institute for Quantitative Research in Economics and Management, Institute Paper No. 16 (1961); L.S. Ritter, "Income Velocity and Anti-Inflationary Monetary Policy," *American Economic Review*, vol. 44 (1954); Richard T. Selden, "Monetary Velocity in the United States," in *Studies in the Quantity Theory of Money*, Milton Friedman, ed. (Chicago: University of Chicago Press, 1956); and Martin Bronfenbrenner and Thomas Mayer, "Liquidity Functions in the American Economy," *Econometrica*, vol. 28 (1960).

Money substitutes and general liquidity were emphasized in the *Report of the Committee on the Working of the Monetary System* (London,: H. M. Stationary Office, 1959), commonly known as the Radcliffe Report; *and* in J. G. Gurley and E. S. Shaw, *Money in a Theory of Finance* (Washington: Brookings, 1960).

cAppendix to Chapter 10

MONEY AND THE BANKING SYSTEM

In this chapter we have assumed that the money supply is an exogenous variable under the control of the central monetary authorities (in the United States, the Federal Reserve Board). Such a description of the money supply would be true only if banks behaved in a very rigid and mechanistic fashion.

Let us examine the behavior of banks. We learn in elementary economics that the banking system can create demand deposits to a multiple of the reserves. This multiple is the reciprocal of the required reserve ratio. If the banking system always created exactly all the deposits it could, then the money supply would be completely within the control of the monetary authorities, who control the reserve ratio by regulation and the quantity of reserves by means of open market policy. Actually, banks sometimes choose to hold excess reserves, that is, they do not make all of the loans which they can. The banks' desire for excess reserves is similar to individuals' desire to hold money for liquidity purposes. It therefore depends on the interest rate and probably has a flat liquidity trap like the liquidity-preference curve of Figure 10.2.

We can describe bank behavior with the following variables and equations.

VARIABLES

Exogenous:

T = Total Reserves
g = Required Reserve Ratio

Endogenous:

D = Demand Deposits
R = Required Reserves
E = Excess Reserves
r = rate of Interest

EQUATIONS

$$gD = R \tag{A10.1}$$
$$R + E = T \tag{A10.2}$$
$$E = E(r) \tag{A10.3}$$
$$T = T_0 \tag{A10.4}$$
$$g = g_0 \tag{A10.5}$$

Equation A10.1 defines required reserves as the amount of demand deposits times the required reserve ratio. Equation A10.2 defines excess reserves as the portion of total reserves not held as backing for deposits. Equation A10.3 is the banks' liquidity function. Equations A10.4 and A10.5 represent the control of total reserves and reserve ratios by the monetary authorities. This system is open, in that there is one more variable than equations.

Given the amount of reserves available (Equation A10.4), banks will decide how much excess reserves they wish to hold (Equation A10.3), and then create deposits by a multiple (Equation A10.1) of the remaining reserves (Equation A10.2). These equations could be summarized into one equation:

$$
\begin{aligned}
D &= \frac{1}{g_0}\,(R) \\
&= \frac{1}{g_0}\,[T_0 - E(r)] \\
&= \frac{1}{g_0}\,T_0 - \frac{1}{g_0}\,E(r) \tag{A10.6}
\end{aligned}
$$

This function can be rearranged as

$$D + \frac{1}{g_0} E(r) = \frac{1}{g_0} T_0 \tag{A10.7}$$

The left side of the equation represents actual deposits created plus the phantom deposits which could have been created had banks not chosen to hold excess reserves. The right-hand side is completely exogenous. If currency were added to both sides, the right side would still consist of exogenous variables and the left would consist of the money supply plus the phantom deposits. If we remember that the money supply is used for transactions and liquidity demand, we find that

$$T(Y) + L(r) + \frac{1}{g_0} E(r) = M_{SP} \tag{A10.8}$$

where M_{SP} represents the *potential* money supply, an exogenous variable. Thus if M_{SP} were substituted for M_S and banks' and individuals' liquidity preferences were added together, the derivation of the *LM* curve remains essentially the same as that of Figure 10.3.

An additional complication arises from the fact that banks have the right to borrow at the Federal Reserve Banks, thereby introducing a measure of their own decision into the size of T, the total reserves. In this case, Equation A10.4 should be replaced by

$$T = O + B \tag{A10.9}$$
$$O = O_0 \tag{A10.10}$$
$$B = B(r,d) \tag{A10.11}$$
$$d = d_0 \tag{A10.12}$$

where O and B represent the banks' owned and borrowed reserves, respectively, and d represents the official rediscount rate. The borrowed reserve function presumably rises as the market rate of interest rises, and declines as the rediscount rate rises. In a sense, borrowed reserves are negative excess reserves, since a bank will not borrow reserves while it still has excess reserves. However, some banks may borrow while others have an excess, so the banking system may have both at once. If these equations are substituted into Equation A10.7 and borrowed reserves are transferred to the left-hand side of the equation, it becomes

$$D + \frac{1}{g_0} E(r) - \frac{1}{g_0} B(r,d_0) = \frac{1}{g_0} O_0 \tag{A10.13}$$

Since borrowed reserves offset excess reserves, the term net free reserves is sometimes used for the net difference. Thus the left-hand side of Equation A10.13 is equal to demand deposits plus the deposits that could have been created from the net free reserves. These free reserves represent the net liquidity position of the banking system. Monetary officials often use their total as a measure of the general stringency of monetary controls and adjust the three policy operations—reserve ratios, rediscount rate, and open-market operations—until the desired level of free reserves has been attained.

cAlgebraic Solutions, *LM* Curve

Again, as in Chapter 9, we have used general functions for liquidity preference and transactions demand. If, however, we assume that these functions are linear, it is easily possible to derive an *LM* curve algebraically. (We will make special allowances for the horizontal and vertical sections of the *LM* curve.) We will use the following equations.

$$M_1 = Y/V \tag{A10.14}$$
$$M_2 = e - dr, \ (M_2 \geq 0, \ r \geq r_0) \tag{A10.15}$$
$$M_1 + M_2 = M_s \tag{A10.16}$$
$$M_s = M_0 \tag{A10.17}$$

Notice that Equation A10.15 is defined only for the range where M_2 is greater than zero and where r is greater than the minimum represented by the liquidity trap. Combining all equations into Equation A10.16, we obtain

$$Y/V + e - dr = M_0 \tag{A10.18}$$

Solving for Y

$$Y = V(dr + M_0 - e)$$
$$= Vdr + VM_0 - eV \tag{A10.19}$$

Applying the conditions of Equation A10.15, we first observe that when M_2 is zero,

$$e = dr \tag{A10.20}$$

Substituting this condition into Equation A10.19 we find

$$Y = Vdr + VM_0 - Vdr$$
$$= VM_0 \qquad \text{(A10.21)}$$

Therefore Equation A10.19 represents the LM curve subject to the two limitations

$$Y \leq VM_0 \qquad \text{(A10.22)}$$
$$r \geq r_0 \qquad \text{(A10.23)}$$

These two limitations indicate that income cannot exceed the level of transactions which can be handled with the money supply, and the interest rate cannot fall below the level of the liquidity trap.

It should be noted that the slope of the LM curve depends upon the product of V and d, the ratio of transactions demand to income and the ratio of liquidity demand to interest rates, respectively.

11

Equilibrium Income

In Chapter 9, the relationship between the rate of interest and the level of income which would provide equilibrium in the commodity market was deduced: the *IS curve*. In Chapter 10, the corresponding relationship in the money market was derived: the *LM curve*. The entire economy is in equilibrium only if both these relationships are satisfied—that is, only if the final combination satisfies both these conditions. To find such a combination, each of these curves is plotted in Figure 11.1. Only the rate of interest r_0 and the national income Y_0 satisfy these conditions; therefore, Y_0 must be the equilibrium national income and r_0 the equilibrium rate of interest consistent with the exogenous variables previously studied.

The systems of Chapter 9 and 10 were both open systems: each contained one more equation than unknown. By combining them, we now have a formally closed system: the number of equations and variables match. We must remember, however, that in a fundamental sense the system is still not closed, for it contains many variables that were specified as exogenous: government spending, taxes, transfers, and the money supply. In addition, each function depends on many unspecified exogenous variables, such as those discussed in Chapters 6 and 7.

Derivation *of* Equilibrium Income

FIGURE 11.1

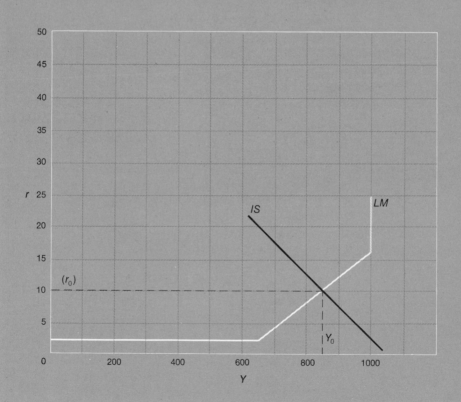

Such a solution can be found numerically as well as graphically. Table 9.2 showed the *IS* curve for the assumed data; Table 10.2, the *LM* curve. These are combined in Table 11.1. From this table, it is clear that both markets are satisfied only at an income of $850 billion and an interest rate of 10 percent.

In order to understand the process by which the society moves to this equilibrium point, it will be necessary to revert to the basic data from which these functions were derived. Table 11.2 shows the derivation of both functions.

Notice that Columns *1* and *2* are the marginal-efficiency-of-capital schedule; Columns *2* and *3*, the equilibrium level of saving; Columns *3* and *4*, the saving function; and Columns *1* and *4*, the *IS* curve. Similarly, Columns *5* and *6* are the transactions demand; *6* and *7*, the equation of money supply and money demand; *7* and *8*, the liquidity-preference schedule, and *5* and *8*, the *LM* curve.

TABLE 11.1

COMPUTATION OF EQUILIBRIUM INCOME
(UNIT: $1 BILLION)

Rate of Interest (%)	Income Which Produces Equilibrium in the Commodity Market[a]	Income Which Produces Equilibrium in the Money Market[b]
20	650	
16		1000
15	750	
14		950
12		900
10	850	850
8		800
6		750
5	950	
4		700
2		650

[a] From Table 9.2.
[b] From Table 10.2.

TABLE 11.2

DERIVATION OF *IS* CURVE AND *LM* CURVE
(UNIT: $1 BILLION)

PART A: *IS* CURVE[a]			
(1)	(2)	(3)	(4)
$r(\%)$	I	$S + (Tx - Tr)$	Y
20	30	160	650
15	70	200	750
10	110	240	850
5	150	280	950

PART B: *LM* CURVE[b]			
(5)	(6)	(7)	(8)
Y	M_1	M_2	$r\ (\%)$
650	117	63	2
700	126	54	4
750	135	45	6
800	144	36	8
850	153	27	10
900	162	18	12
950	171	9	14

[a] $G_0 = 130; Tx_0 - Tr_0 = 100.$
[b] $M_s = 180.$

Let us examine the process of adjustment from a position that is not the equilibrium. Suppose we started at an income of $800 billion and an interest rate of 8 percent: This position is consistent with equilibrium in the money market (*LM* curve), but not with equilibrium in the commodity market (*IS* curve). Let us follow the reaction

𝓔quilibrium in Both Markets

FIGURE 11.2

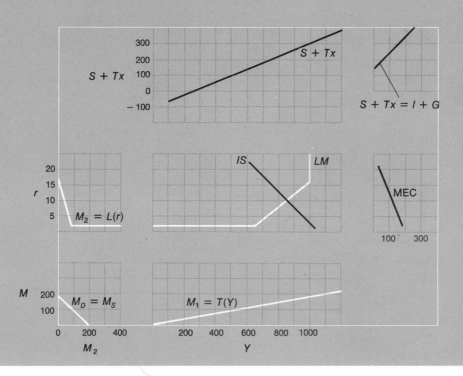

by interpolating the necessary values. At an interest rate of 8 percent, business would invest $126 billion. This investment, coupled with the assumed constant government spending of $130 billion, would require leakages of $256 billion and an expansion of income to $890 billion. With an interest rate of 8 percent, this income is consistent with the *IS* curve, but now the money market is out of adjustment.

An income of $890 billion would require $160.2 billion for transactions purposes, leaving $19.8 billion for idle balances. Competition for this sum would drive interest rates to 11.6 percent. The money market is now back in adjustment, but the commodity market must begin a new round. This round would end with income at $818 billion. A further round of adjustment in the money market would lower interest rates to 8.7 percent. Successive rounds of adjustment would finally lead to the equilibrium values of 10 percent and an income of $850 billion. The purpose of following through this process of adjustment is to see the relation of this equilibrium value to the behavior of individuals in the society. This description is, obviously, very rigid in its summary of behavior, for the adjustments ordinarily take place simultaneously in both markets. Such simultaneous action will diminish the probability of fluctuations and permit the society to creep up on its equilibrium level.

It is possible to combine the graphic derivations of the *IS* curve and the *LM* curve into one summary graph. The *IS* curve is the lower left-hand corner of Figure 9.1; the *LM* curve is the upper right-hand corner of Figure 10.3. These entire graphs can be superimposed as shown in Figure 11.2. The four graphs in the upper right describe the commodity market; the four in the lower left, the money market.

𝒯𝔥𝔢 Multipliers Again

In Chapters 4 and 5, various multipliers were computed, showing the reaction of national income to changes in government expenditures and other variables. In each of these multipliers it was assumed, however, that investment remained fixed at some previously determined level. The analysis of this chapter indicates that such an assumption is unrealistic. An increase in income would have repercussions in the money market, raising the rate of interest. This higher

The Multiplier and Actual Income Changes

FIGURE 11.3

Multiplier Change: Y_0 *to* Y_2

Actual Change: Y_0 *to* Y_1

Dampening Effect of Change in Interest Rate: Y_2 *to* Y_1

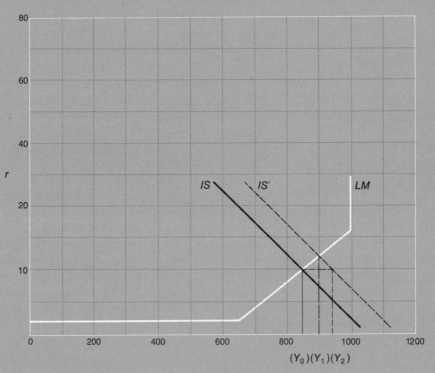

$(Y_0)(Y_1)(Y_2)$

Y

rate of interest would decrease the amount of investment and thereby keep income from rising as far as it otherwise would. If the *LM* curve were horizontal, the increase in income would not affect the interest rate. In such a case, the multiplier would give an accurate picture of the increase in income. In all other cases, the actual increase in income would be less than that given by the multiplier. Figure 11.3 illustrates the difference between these shifts. *IS'* represents the new *IS* curve after an increase in government spending.

cAn Example: Increased Government Spending

As an indication of the repercussions that would take place throughout the economy as the result of a change in one factor, let us examine the effects of increased government expenditures. Let us assume an increase of $36 billion. The multiplier being $2\frac{1}{2}$, the *IS* curve moves to the right $90 billion. This new *IS* curve intersects the *LM* curve at an income of $900 billion and an interest rate of 12 percent. Such a shift is illustrated in Figure 11.4.

From an examination of the new equilibrium position, we can see that investment has fallen from $110 to $94 billion, government spending has risen from $130 to $166 billion, and total leakages have risen from $240 to $260 billion. In the money market, the money supply has been reallocated, with $162 billion being used for transactions, M_1, and $18 billion for liquidity, M_2, as compared with the previous values of $153 billion and $27 billion, respectively.

The student should test his understanding of this process by examining the effects of changes in all the basic functions on the rate of interest, income, saving, investment, active balances, and passive balances. He should be prepared to discuss the effect of an increase (or decrease) in the marginal efficiency of capital, government spending, the saving function, taxes, liquidity preference, the transactions demand, and the supply of money. Note that in each case, the emphasis is on the effects of *shifts* in curves, not movements along the curves.

The Effect of Increased Government Spending

FIGURE 11.4

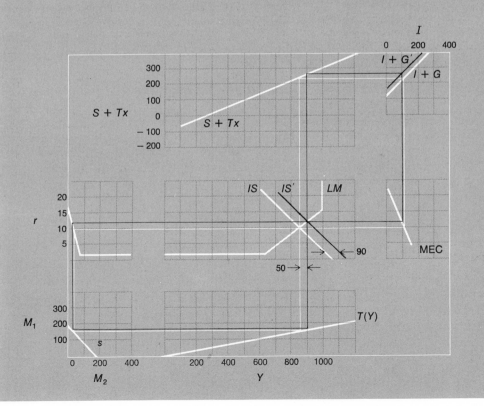

PROBLEMS AND DISCUSSION QUESTIONS

1. Using the data of Problem 1, Chapter 9, and Problem 3, Chapter 10, find the equilibrium income and interest rate. Find the equilibrium values of I, S, M_1 and M_2.

2. Using these same data, find the effect of an increase in the money supply to $325 billion. What would be the new equilibrium values of r, I, Y, S, M_1 and M_2?

3. (*For those who read the Appendixes to Chapters 9 and 10*) Combine the algebraic derivations of the *IS* and *LM* curves to find the equilibrium income. Use the numerical examples at the end of each chapter to obtain coefficients for all the equations and obtain a numerical solution.

SUGGESTED ADDITIONAL READINGS

An alternative approach to the relation of the multiplier and the money market can be found in L. S. Ritter, "Some Monetary Aspects of Multiplier Theory and Fiscal Policy," *Review of Economic Studies*, vol. 23, (1956).

12

cAggregate Demand

The previous chapters have dealt with the various factors that influence the aggregate demand for goods and services and the effect of each on the level of aggregate demand. Now the effects of price changes must be considered. In preceding chapters, we have been examining elements that *shift* the demand curve; we now want to see what shape the demand curve has as we move *along* it to a different price. This order is the opposite of that usually followed in discussing the demand for a specific product; the price usually is considered first, then the factors that shift the curve. There are two reasons for the present reversal of order. The first is simplicity: The analysis of price changes involves many of the elements that have been previously discussed. It is, therefore, easier to discuss price changes now, after the study of the other details of aggregate demand.

The second reason is institutional. In a society like that of the United States, there are substantial elements of monopoly and tradition. These are evident both in product markets and in labor markets. Where such elements exist, prices tend to have a certain rigidity and often change in jumps rather than smoothly. It is, therefore, a reasonably accurate description to say that *usually* the supply curve seems to be flat, at least if there is significant unemployment, and shifts in demand alter real national product, not its price. We have therefore concentrated first on those shifts in demand and the forces behind them.

We do observe, however, that prices do change over time. A complete understanding of the forces affecting national product and income requires that we give some attention to the role of price. In this chapter we will concentrate on price in its relation to aggregate demand; in the next chapter we will look at aggregate supply. For the moment, the system is again open and price is an exogenous variable.

The Keynes Effect

The question of the effect of price changes upon aggregate demand has an important place in discussions of antidepression policy. Many businessmen and some economists argue that a depression could be stopped if only workers would agree to accept reduced wages. Lower wages, they claim, would lower business costs and induce greater output. This would certainly be true of any single firm or industry whose workers would accept lower wages; it should therefore be true of the whole society. This argument is based upon the classical system outlined in Chapter 3.

Other economists argue that this view is a delusion. If the workers of one firm accept reduced wages, there will be little or no change in the demand of that firm, since most of the customers are not employees. But if all firms cut wages, the demand would fall, since the employees of one firm are the customers of others. The net effect would be merely a lower wage level and price level, but no change in the total amount of sales. (It is true that there might be some flurry of increased output after wages fell and before prices fell, but the increase would be only temporary.)

Keynes, in his *General Theory*, discussed this problem. In effect, he considered each of the functions involved in determining aggregate demand to see if price had any effect. Let us follow his reasoning.

The marginal efficiency of capital is based upon the relative size of present costs and future returns. If prices fall and are expected to stay at the new level, then future returns fall in exactly the same degree. If there is no change in interest rates, the investments that were previously profitable are still profitable. So long as the dollar value of investment is adjusted for price changes, there will be no change in the marginal efficiency of capital.

If the government is buying a certain set of goods and services, then government expenditures rise with prices. If Congress votes a pay increase, it must vote a corresponding increase in the budget.

Keynes's discussion of the consumption function follows along similar lines. He believed that consumers made their decisions on the basis of purchasing power. Thus, if incomes and prices fall uniformly, there is no reason to assume that consumers will change their actual purchases, although the dollar value of the purchases would fall. (Remember that we agreed in Chapter 2 to measure all these factors in real terms, adjusted for prices. There will therefore be no change in these adjusted measurements.)

Since these three relationships, investment, government spending, and consumption, constitute the description of the commodity market, Keynes concluded that there would be no change in the position of the *IS* curve as a result of changes in price level.

In examining the demand for money, one should expect to find the same phenomenon. If all prices are lower, less money will be needed to finance day-to-day transactions. Similarly, one should expect investors' liquidity preference to be stated in terms of purchasing power. Thus, the demand for money remains unchanged after adjustment for price changes.

There remains only the supply of money. Here, however, one notices a change as the price level changes. As prices fall, incomes and consumptions may fall, but a dollar bill remains a dollar bill. If the money supply is $180 billion and the price level falls to half its former level, the purchasing power of the money supply becomes $360 billion. We would expect, therefore, a lower price to have the same effect as an increase in the money supply.

An increase in the money supply has the effect of shifting the *LM* curve to the right. Thus, a lower price would have the same effect. As the *LM* curve shifts the interest rate will fall and income will increase. These effects are shown in Figure 12.1.

As the illustration shows, when the price falls from P_1 to P_2, the effective money supply increases to about $212 billion, the interest rate falls from 10 percent to about 6 percent, and real income increases to about $930 billion. As the price falls still further, to P_3, the interest rate falls to 2 percent and real income rises just over $1000 billion. However, as the price falls below P_3, the only changes that would take place in the *LM* curve are beyond the intersection with the *IS* curve. This is so because in these graphs 2 percent is the minimal

The Keynes Effect

FIGURE 12.1

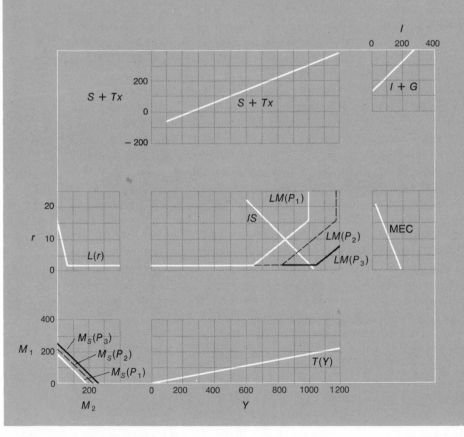

interest rate. In Chapter 10, it was observed that, at some low interest rate, security-holders are willing to hold any amount of money rather than to bid down interest rates any further. In Figure 12.1, 2 percent is that bottom rate.

Table 12.1 shows the derivation of the *LM* curve for two price levels. The basic data for the transactions demand for money and liquidity preference are the same as those of Table 10.1.

If an *LM* curve is derived using the $P = 100$ column of Table 12.1, the same result is obtained as in Chapter 10. For example, at an income of \$800 billion, \$144 billion are required for M_1. This leaves \$36 billion to satisfy liquidity preference and forces interest rates to 8 percent. The complete schedule is given in Table 12.2.

TABLE 12.1

THE KEYNES EFFECT
(UNIT: \$1 BILLION)

PART A Transactions Demand for Money		PART B Money Demand Equals Money Supply[a]				PART C Liquidity Preference	
		$P = 100$		$P = 72$			
Y	M_1	M_1	M_2	M_1	M_2	$r\ (\%)$	M_2
650	117	117	63	117	133	2	63 or more
700	126	126	54	126	124	4	54
750	135	135	45	135	115	6	45
800	144	144	36	144	106	8	36
850	153	153	27	153	97	10	27
900	162	162	18	162	88	12	18
950	171	171	9	171	79	14	9
1000	180	180	0	180	70	16	0
1050	189			189	61		

[a] Money supply = \$180 billion.

TABLE 12.2

LM CURVES
(UNIT: $1 BILLION)

P = 100		P = 72	
Y	r (%)	Y	r (%)
650	2	750	2
700	4	800	2
750	6	850	2
800	8	900	2
850	10	950	2
900	12	1000	2
950	14	1050	2+

When price falls to 72, the effective money supply rises to $250 billion. At all income levels below $1040 billion, there is still more than $63 billion available to satisfy liquidity preference. Thus the interest rate remains at the 2 percent minimum. This *LM* curve is also shown in Table 12.2.

Thus a decline in prices tends to force the *LM* curve to the right. This moves the intersection with the *IS* curve to a lower interest rate and higher income unless the interest rate is already at the minimal level, in which case price changes have no further effect.

The aggregate demand curve that results from this analysis is shown in Figure 12.2. The real income demanded never exceeds the level shown by the *IS* curve at the minimal rate of interest. In this example, the level is $1010 billion.

It can now be seen why the analysis of liquidity preference and the *liquidity trap* was such an important part of Keynes's attack on the classical system. In classical economics, price *always* had an effect. Since classical economics did not allow for liquidity preference, the *LM* curve was always vertical, just as it was in the example of interest rates above 14 percent: the level at which M_2 became zero. If the *LM* curve was vertical, shifts to the right would result in lower interest rates and increased investment. Thus a decline in the price level would always restore full employment.

Aggregate Demand Curve (Keynes Effect)

FIGURE 12.2

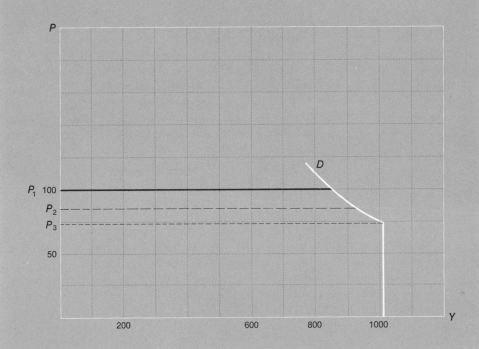

Basing his argument on the *liquidity trap,* Keynes argued that there were limits beyond which aggregate demand would not increase, however low the price. It was quite possible that this limit might not be enough to provide jobs for all who were willing to work. If the unemployed tried to obtain work by bidding down wages, other people might become unemployed, but total employment would not change. Keynes, therefore, proposed that depressions be fought by government spending, thereby *shifting* aggregate demand by shifting the *IS* curve, rather than by placing faith in expansion through lowered prices.

The Pigou Effect

Keynes's conclusions were unacceptable to two groups. The first group objected because his analysis made government intervention or continued depression the only two possible alternatives. Many members of this group opposed government intervention on principle and therefore rejected this choice as undesirable.

The second group, the supporters of classical analysis, opposed Keynes's conclusions on logical rather than political grounds. To them, it seemed impossible that workers could not find jobs by cutting their wages sufficiently. Among this group was A. C. Pigou, who discussed the question in his article "The Classical Stationary State." He observed that price changes would alter the consumption function. This reaction has become to be known as the *Pigou effect* or, because it depends on the real value of consumer balances, the *real balance effect.*

In Chapter 6 we mentioned the role of consumer assets as determinants of consumption. An increase in consumer assets tends to increase the willingness of consumers to spend their current income for consumption. A decline in prices tends to raise the value of money assets and, therefore, to raise the consumption function.

Let us consider in detail the effects upon consumers of a change in prices. As prices fall, incomes tend to fall proportionately. Thus a consumer with no assets finds himself in the same position as before the decline in prices. Even if he has durable consumer assets, they decline in money value with price. The same is usually true of stocks.

Only bonds and cash tend to maintain their money value, which means a rise in purchasing power. This increase in purchasing power tends to raise consumption and lower saving.

To illustrate, let us imagine a very simplified example. Suppose that an individual has a disposable income of $5000 per year and expects to work for thirty years. He would like to have a retirement fund equal to six years' income. Accordingly, each year he spends $4000 for consumption and saves $1000. By the end of ten years, he has saved $10,000. Now suppose that prices, and his income, are cut in half. He now earns $2500 and can buy the same consumption goods as before for $2000. But what about his saving needs? His retirement goal of six years' income is now $15,000. Since he has twenty years to go, he can reach the goal by saving $250 each year. Thus, he can maintain his old consumption level and achieve his old saving goal for $2250—less than his income. He will probably spend at least a part of the extra $250 on consumption, thus raising his standard of living and his consumption function. This increase in consumption is possible because the fall in price has put him ten years ahead on his saving program.

The rise in the consumption function associated with a lower price level means a lower saving function. The fall in the saving function moves the IS curve to the right, increasing the rate of interest and level of income. An example is shown in Figure 12.3.

Since there are no flat portions of the IS curve, there is no limit to the amount of expansion of aggregate demand that can come about through the Pigou effect. The aggregate demand curve has the shape indicated in Figure 12.4.

This result satisfied Pigou. He had proved that it was always possible to obtain full employment if wages and prices fell sufficiently. As a logical proposition, this conclusion was almost indisputable, and Pigou claimed nothing more than logic. Strangely enough, this result also satisfied the political opponents of Keynes, who could now blame unemployment on the unwillingness of workers to accept lower wages, for Pigou had shown that there exists *some* level of wages that would be compatible with full employment. The important practical question was an empirical one: just how elastic is the aggregate supply curve? If the elasticity is very high, a modest change in price might produce the desired income level. If the elasticity is low, the price level that is compatible with full employment might require such a large change that the process of reaching it would be hopelessly disruptive. (Imagine what would happen if it were necessary to lower the price level to one tenth its present level.)

The question of how much prices must change to produce a given

The Pigou Effect

FIGURE 12.3

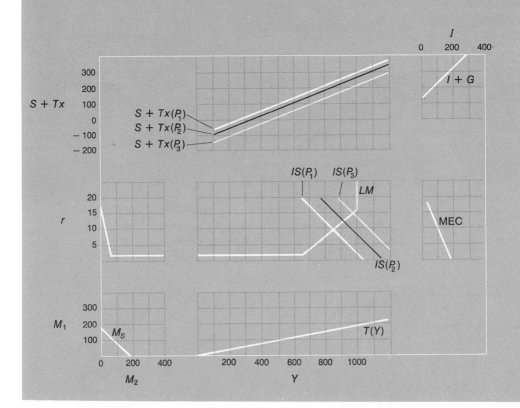

Aggregate
Demand Curve
(Pigou Effect)

FIGURE 12.4

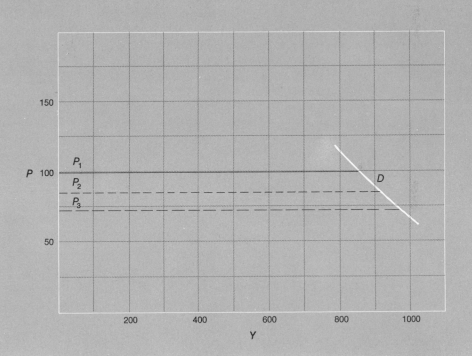

level of income cannot be answered by any purely theoretical analysis. Only statistical study, concerned with the size of consumer assets and debts and the effects of these upon consumption, could offer even a tentative hypothesis. The usual conclusion is that very large changes in prices would be required for moderate changes in income. Nevertheless, the controversy is not yet settled, and further study continues.

The Aggregate Demand Curve

To obtain an aggregate demand curve, the Pigou effect and the Keynes effect must be combined. We choose a price at random. For this price there is a corresponding effective money supply and a specific consumption function. Using these functions, we draw the appropriate *IS* and *LM* curves. Their intersection gives the corresponding income. If this process is repeated for other prices, other incomes are obtained. Connecting these gives the aggregate demand curve. Such a process is shown in Figure 12.5.

Figure 12.5 shows that decreases in price cause an increase in aggregate demand—that is, in national income. It is impossible to foretell the net effect of the price change on the interest rate. The Keynes effect tends to lower the interest rate; the Pigou effect tends to raise the interest rate. The net result of both might be in the direction of either higher or lower interest rates, depending upon the relative size of the two effects.

Prices Changed and Changing

The analysis of this chapter deals with the level of aggregate demand at various price levels. It was seen that lower prices mean higher aggregate demand. In dealing with aggregate demand as well as with the demand for individual products, one must distinguish this effect

Derivation of Aggregate Demand Curve

FIGURE 12.5

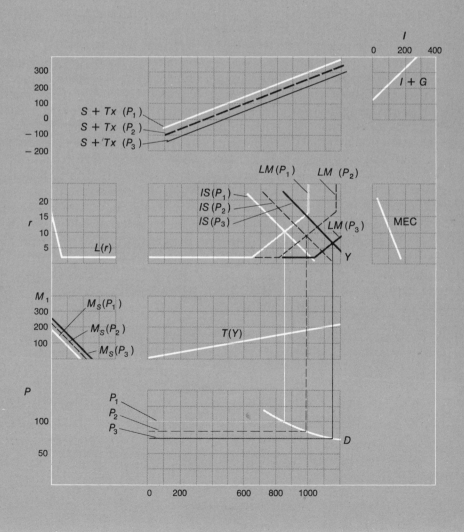

from the analysis of falling prices. If prices are falling and people expect them to fall even further, consumers and investors will postpone their purchases until prices reach the lowest level. This is especially true of the purchases of durable and semidurable goods that can be postponed. Similarly, although *higher* prices discourage spending, *rising* prices encourage it if they create the expectation of further increases.

The problem of expectation affects all aspects of the analysis of aggregate demand. If prices fall but are expected to rise later, investment might be encouraged, since present costs decline but future revenue does not. In such circumstances, however, the Pigou effect would not operate, for individuals would not revalue their assets. If one expects to spend his assets only after retirement, he will revalue them only if he expects prices in the future to be different. A temporary fall in price will, therefore, cause no re-evaluation of assets and, consequently, no change in consumption. In some cases, a temporary fall might even cause a decrease in consumption. Some forms of saving, especially through insurance or payroll-deduction plans, tend to be fixed in dollars. A decline in prices and income would leave these programs unaffected; therefore less money would be available for consumption. If the price decline were permanent, these programs would probably be rewritten, but a temporary decline would not induce such revision. Thus, a temporary fall might tend to decrease consumption although a permanent fall would tend to increase it.

For all these reasons, one must be very careful in using this analysis to describe dynamic processes. It is intended to describe only the effects of *different* levels of price, not the movement *between* them.

PROBLEMS AND DISCUSSION QUESTIONS

1. Is the Pigou effect apt to be more or less important now than in the past? Why?

2. From your own observation, estimate the size of the Pigou effect. Does this estimate give you much faith in its efficacy in preventing depression?

3. From a current *Federal Reserve Bulletin*, find the rate of interest on the most recent issue of long-term governmental securities. What do you conclude from this about the strength of the Keynes effect:

4. On the basis of your answer to Problem 3, what is the shape of the aggregate demand curve?

5. From the discussion in Chapter 7 on factors affecting investment, we saw that availability of funds encourages investment. Analyze the way in which changed price levels would affect the balance sheet of a firm. Is there a "real balance" effect on investment? Is it positive or negative?

SUGGESTED ADDITIONAL READINGS

The Keynes effect is set forth in J. M. Keynes, *The General Theory of Employment, Interest and Money,* Chapter 19. The Pigou effect is described in A. C. Pigou, "The Classical Stationary State," *Economic Journal* (1943), and in "Economic Progress in a Stable Environment," *Economica* (1947), reprinted in *Readings in Monetary Theory* (Homewood, Ill.: Richard D. Irwin, Inc., 1951). *See also* Keynes, *General Theory,* Parag. 3, pp. 92–93, as a possible forerunner of Pigou.

On the general subject of price flexibility and aggregate demand, *see* James Tobin, "Money Wage Rates and Employment," in Seymour Harris, *The New Economics* (New York: Knopf, 1950), or "Asset Holdings and Spending Decisions," *American Economic Review, Papers and Proceedings*, vol. 42 (1952). This subject was also explored by Don Patinkin, "Prince Flexibility and Full Employment," *American Economic Review,* vol. 38 (1948), reprinted in *Readings in Monetary Theory.*

For a later discussion, *see* Thomas Mayer, "The Empirical Significance of the Real Balance Effect," *Quarterly Journal of Economics,* vol. 73 (1959).

13

$\mathcal{A}$ggregate Supply

In the recent analysis of national income and product, economists have given most of their attention to the determinants of aggregate demand, with relatively little attention to aggregate supply. In part, this neglect was a reaction to the classical emphasis on aggregate supply and neglect of aggregate demand. In part, it reflected a view that one can treat the aggregate supply curve as perfectly horizontal up to full employment and practically vertical thereafter. The main reason for neglecting the aggregate supply curve is the feeling that it is already adequately understood. Since the aggregate is believed to be almost exactly the same as the supply curve of an individual product, there is no need for especial elaboration.

In order to understand the conditions of supply, let us briefly review the analysis of the behavior of a single firm. The objective of the firm is to make as much profit as possible. It will be assumed that the firm is purely competitive, so that it is faced with a given price and a given wage over which it has no control. In order to maximize its profits, the firm must adjust its level of production—the only variable within its control. Since we are considering only short-run analysis, the firm's output will depend upon the inputs of the variable factors of production, especially labor. Capital equipment and other fixed factors of production are not variable in the short run.

Imagine that this firm has a schedule by which it knows the amount of output it can obtain from any given input of labor. In order to tell whether to hire an additional worker, it must compare the value of the added (or marginal) product with the added cost of hiring the worker. This is merely another way of stating the principle that firms adjust their production until marginal cost equals marginal revenue. The marginal revenue is the marginal product times the price.

This same result can be obtained in another way. If a worker can produce 100 units of output per week and his wage is only 80 times the price of the unit of output, hiring him yields a profit of 20 units of output. Firms will continue to expand until the marginal output of the last worker is only as high as the number of units of output that his wage will buy.

In progressing from a single firm to an entire industry, the same principles apply. The only difference is that more workers are employed, and more output is produced; but the same ratios among wages, prices, and marginal product exist.

In going from an industry to the nation the same principles are used, but special techniques of measurement are applied. No longer can output be measured by means of simple quantity or simple price. We must measure national output in terms of real national income and price by using a price index. (By *the* wage rate, is meant merely an average of all rates, and this is used as an index of labor costs.)

Let us then list the variables and relationships that are required to determine the aggregate supply curve. (As was done before, general functions are used when there is not enough information to give an exact relationship.)

VARIABLES

Endogenous:

Y = Real Income = National Product

N = Employment

$\dfrac{\Delta Y}{\Delta N}$ = Marginal Product

w = Real Wage

Exogenous:

P = General Price Level

w^* = Money Wage Rate

EQUATIONS

$$w = \frac{w^*}{P} \tag{13.1}$$

$$w = \frac{\Delta Y}{\Delta N} \tag{13.2}$$

$$Y = F(N) \text{ (Production Function)} \tag{13.3}$$

$$\frac{\Delta Y}{\Delta N} = F'(N) \text{ (Marginal Productivity)} \tag{13.4}$$

$$w^* = w^*_0 \tag{13.5}$$

These equations restate the principles given above for profit maximization. Equation 13.1 defines real wage as the money wage divided by the price level. Equation 13.2 is the condition for profit maximization: marginal product must equal the real cost of hiring the worker, the real wage. Equation 13.3 shows that the national product depends upon the number of people employed. The marginal product (which is the increase in real income per additional worker) can be derived from the production function $F(N)$. Equation 13.4 records this relationship, using $F'(N)$ to indicate the marginal-productivity function. Finally, Equation 13.5 shows that the money wage is a factor beyond the scope of the present discussion. Some of the problems of its determination will be discussed later. Since there are six variables here and only five equations, we again have an open system, in which price is an exogenous variable. The system will be closed only in the last section of the chapter where aggregate supply will be combined with the aggregate demand curve of Chapter 12.

The derivation of such a supply curve is shown in Table 13.1. Part A corresponds to Equation 13.1; Part B, to Equation 13.4; and Part C to Equation 13.3. Part B is derived from Part C. For each employment level, we measure the increase in output which accompanies the last increase in employment and divide the two increases to find the marginal product per worker. In the simplified example given here, the increases are measured in units of 10 million men, but they would normally be measured in much smaller units.

In order to derive an aggregate supply curve, we begin with a price level chosen at random—say 100 percent. At that level, a money wage of \$9000 means a real wage of \$9000 in purchasing power (Part A). Since the profit-maximizing rule of Equation 13.2 says that the real wage should equal the marginal product, we search for a marginal product of \$9000. We find such productivity at an employment of 70 million men (Part B). The production function (Part C) tells

TABLE 13.1

DERIVATION OF AGGREGATE SUPPLY CURVE

PART A		PART B		PART C	
The Real Wage[a]		Marginal Productivity		Production Function	
P (%)	w	N (in millions)	$\dfrac{\Delta Y}{\Delta N}$	N (in millions)	Y (in billions)
70	$12,857	10	$16,000	10	$160
80	11,250	20	14,000	20	300
90	10,000	30	13,000	30	430
100	9000	40	12,000	40	550
110	8182	50	11,000	50	660
		60	10,000	60	760
		70	9000	70	850
		80	8000	80	930

[a] Assuming a money wage of $9000.

us that 70 million men can produce an output of $850 billion, measured at base year prices. Thus we have found that, at a price level of 100 percent, total product supplied will be $850 billion. Using other prices, we can find other points on the supply curve, which is given in Table 13.2. (In order to find exact points, it would be necessary to add some intermediate values to one or more parts of Table 13.1.) Such a supply curve might properly be considered Part D of Table 13.1.

The same analysis is shown in graphic form in Figure 13.1. Each part of the figure corresponds to a part of Table 13.1. Starting with a price chosen at random, we find the corresponding real wage in Part (A). In Part (B) we find the level of employment for which the marginal product is equal to that wage. Part (C) gives the national product corresponding to that level of employment. This product is plotted in Part (D) opposite the starting price. Repeating

The Aggregate Supply Curve

FIGURE 13.1

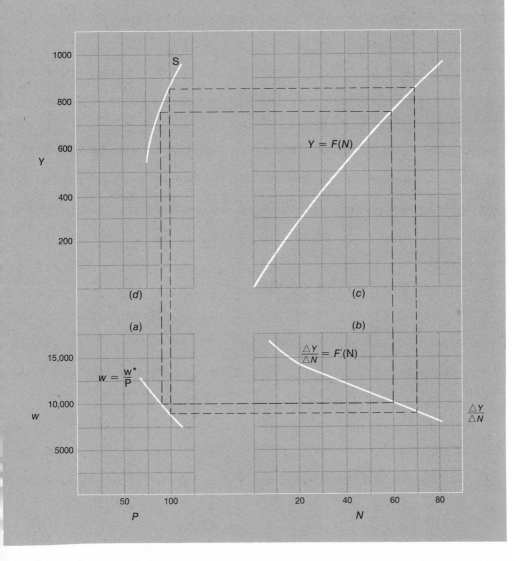

TABLE 13.2

HYPOTHETICAL AGGREGATE SUPPLY CURVE

P (%)	Y (in billions)
75.0	$550
81.8	660
90.0	760
100.0	850
112.5	930

the process gives the aggregate supply curve. Note that the axes of the aggregate supply curve are reversed from those of the aggregate demand curve in Chapter 12.

It would be well to pause at this point to emphasize once again the assumptions that underlie this analysis. It has been assumed that the level of employment depends upon the desires of employers— that is, that the labor supply always exceeds the demand for labor. Such is usually the case at less than full employment.

More important is the assumption of pure competition. Some economists have argued that our economy is almost purely competitive. They find the differences between the actual results and those of a purely competitive society negligible. If this analysis is correct, the assumption yields the correct results. For the skeptical (including the author), this analysis should be regarded merely as a preliminary step to the more advanced discussion below.

Excise Taxes and Supply Curve

Excise or sales taxes have the same effect on the aggregate supply curve as on the supply curve of an individual product. The tax creates a difference between the price paid by customers and the amount received by producers. In order to determine the quantity of goods

Excise Taxes and Supply

FIGURE 13.2

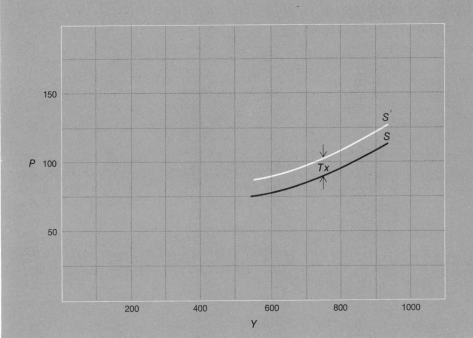

which will be supplied at a given price, it is necessary to subtract the sales tax to find the producers' receipts. Then the analysis follows the lines given above. Figure 13.2 shows the adjustment for taxes: the lower curve indicates supply without tax, and the upper curve indicates the supply with imposition of tax.

In practice, the analysis is not quite as simple, since many of our taxes are not imposed uniformly on all products. Many state sales taxes exempt certain kinds of products. The federal excise-tax structure is a collection of varying rates established according to revenue needs, characteristics of particular industries, and equity considerations. However, at any given level of national income, the distribution of purchases among the various industries will be approximately given, so that the amount of excise tax can be estimated for every level of national income. From these estimates, it is possible to construct a relation between an aggregate supply curve including excise taxes and the aggregate supply curve excluding taxes. However, in this case S' would not be a uniform distance from S, but would vary according to the amount of tax at that level of income.

$\mathcal{M}$onopoly

In our society, there are a number of elements of monopoly and monopolistic practice. In analyzing pure competition, attention can be confined to price; in monopoly, the marginal revenue differs from price. It is often said, in this sense, that a monopolist has no supply curve, because the amount he will sell depends not only upon the price, but upon the shape of the demand curve as well.

It is possible to construct an aggregate supply curve even though individual supply curves cannot be constructed. In order to do this, we use the same kind of reasoning that was used for excise taxes. For every level of national income, there is a specific distribution of the product among various industries. For each industry that is monopolized, there exists some ratio between marginal revenue and price. (As price and marginal revenue are the same in competitive industries, the ratio is one.) By taking a weighted average of these ratios, a ratio between marginal revenue and price can be obtained for the entire society at every income level. The supply depends upon

Monopoly and Aggregate Supply

FIGURE 13.3

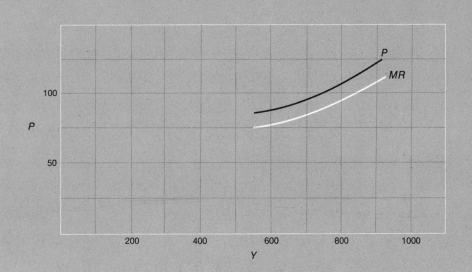

the marginal revenue, but purchases depend upon the price. Figure 13.3 shows the relationship between these two curves. The curve labeled MR is the same as the supply curve previously derived; the curve labeled P is obtained simply by increasing the level of the MR curve by the ratio of price to marginal revenue. An increase in the degree of monopoly will widen the gap. Again, the distance between these curves need not be uniform.

For those who prefer to think of it in this fashion, the presence of the monopoly has the same effect on the supply curve as the imposition of a sales tax. In this case, however, the tax is imposed by the monopolist, not the government. An increase in the degree of monopoly is the same as an increase in the tax.

Say's Law Again

It has been assumed so far that there is no competition in the labor market, so that the wage remains fixed regardless of the level of employment. If, on the other hand, we assume perfect competition in the labor market, we would be returning to the assumptions underlying Say's law. In order to analyze such a situation, we need to make certain changes in our previous analysis. These changes are shown in Figure 13.4.

In this case, we have retained Parts (B) and (C) of Figure 13.1. However, we have added to Part (B) a supply curve of labor to match the marginal productivity curve that represents the demand for labor. As long as there is unemployment, workers will bid money wages down until the real wage has reached the equilibrium level (in this case $9000 at base prices). If there are unfilled jobs, employers will bid the wage up. This determines employment at 70 million workers and output of $850 billion. There is no need for Part (A) in this diagram, because the money wage is not considered fixed. If we wished, we might put in a new Part (A) with a whole family of curves, representing different money wages. We could then use w, determined from Part (B), and P, determined from Part (D), to find the required money wage. However, it is simpler just to use the definition

$$w^* = Pw \qquad (13.6)$$

The Classical Supply Curve

FIGURE 13.4

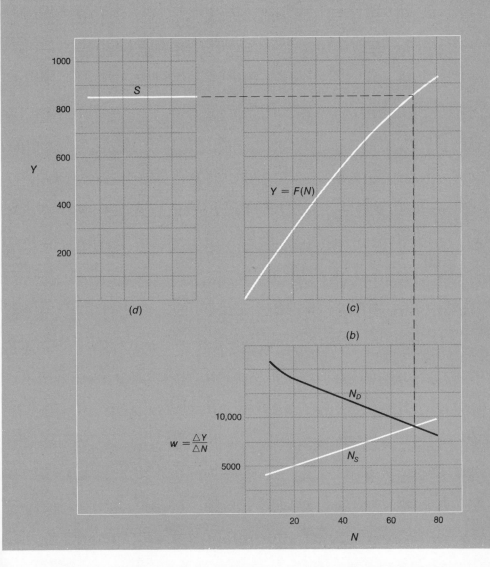

Aggregate Supply Curve with Partly Variable Wages

FIGURE 13.5

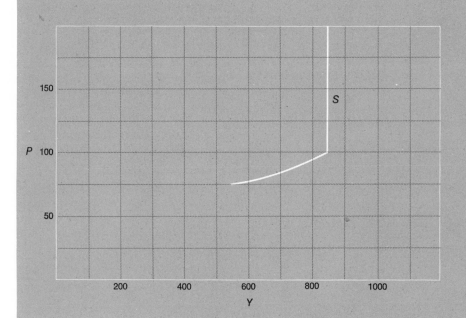

The money wage can be determined by multiplying the real wage by the price level.

The question then arises: which is more realistic, Figure 13.1, with fixed wages, or Figure 13.4, with variable wages? Many people have argued that Figure 13.1 is more realistic in case of unemployment, but that wages are flexible upward. Employers are apt to bid wages up to try to fill jobs as prices rise. In this case, the aggregate supply curve would be a hybrid, reflecting fixed wages up to full employment and flexible wages beyond. Such a curve is shown in Figure 13.5.

The argument presented here indicates that there is a long-run pressure in favor of higher wages. If workers resist wage cuts, even at the cost of unemployment, wages will remain steady in bad times. If employers would rather pay higher wages than have unfilled jobs, wages will rise in good times. A discussion of wages and inflation is given in Chapter 16, but it can be seen now that wages have a general tendency to upward bias.

Supply and Demand

To find the final equilibrium of supply and demand, we combine the results of previous chapters. If the aggregate demand curve of Chapter 12 and the aggregate supply curve of Chapter 13 are put together, the final equilibrium values of the price level and of real national income can be found. Such a process is shown in Figure 13.6.

Here, a summary of those variables that are included in this system but that have not been explained must be given. In the demand system are the three government fiscal variables—government expenditures, transfers, and taxes—the money supply, and the assets in the hands of consumers. This last variable is essentially the result of history— particularly, of the saving history of consumers. In the supply system, the principal unexplained variable is the money wage rate. Changes in any of these variables will change the equilibrium level of prices and of income. If there was enough information about all the relevant functions, the direction and magnitude of the change could be computed from this system.

In addition to these omitted variables, of course, any change in

Aggregate Supply and Demand

FIGURE 13.6

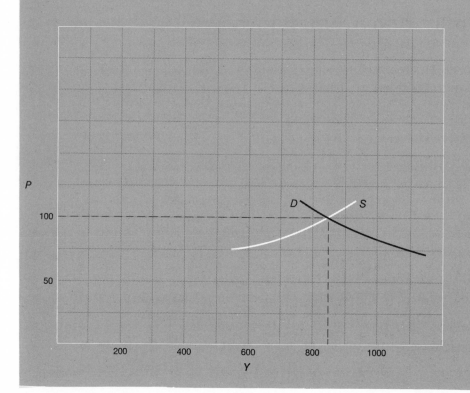

Aggregate Supply and Demand and Their Components

FIGURE 13.7

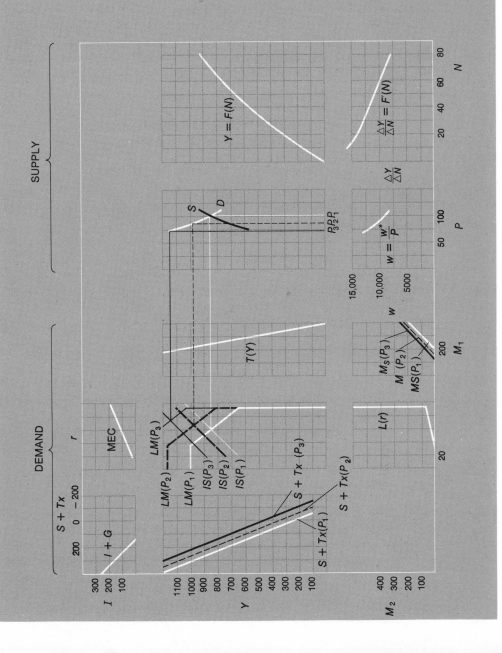

one of the component functions (consumption function, and the like) will change these equilibrium values.

The relation of all the component functions to these summary supply and demand curves is shown in Figure 13.7. This figure is a summary diagram, covering the general outlines of the analysis given previously. The demand portions repeat Figure 12.5; the supply portions repeat Figure 13.1. The appropriate adjustments to account for increased government spending or to allow for the influence of labor market conditions could be made by the use of other figures as the models for the parts of this one. All the analysis of this book can be summarized in this one graph, but all the qualifications given throughout the text also apply to it.

PROBLEMS AND DISCUSSION QUESTIONS

1. The production function is as follows:

N	Y
10	$200
20	380
30	540
40	680
50	800
60	900
70	980

The money wage in $10,000 per year. Find the aggregate supply curve.

2. What is the equilibrium level of income and prices if the aggregate demand is:

P	Y
150	900
125	980
100	1060
75	1140

Interpolate as necessary.

3. If all labor had *escalator clauses* making money wages directly responsive to the cost of living, what would the effect be on aggregate supply? Would you consider this effect good?

4. How realistic do you consider the assumptions made in the text about wage policy of employers and workers? If you were to alter these assumptions, what would be the resultant supply curve?

5. If excise taxes were levied most heavily on luxuries, how would the supply curve be affected?

6. Would you expect an increase or a decrease in P, Y, N, I, and C to result from:

    a. increased marginal efficiency of capital?

    b. decreased money supply?

    c. decreased money wages?

    d. technological progess?

    e. increased government spending?

    f. rise in consumption function?

SUGGESTED ADDITIONAL READINGS

The analysis of this chapter is merely an extension of the theory of the firm in pure competition which can be found in any principle textbook. More precisely, it is adapted from O. H. Brownlee, "Money, Price Level, and Employment," in *Applied Economic Analysis*, Francis M. Boddy, ed. (New York: Pitman, 1948).

14

Classical and Keynesian *A*nalysis

Having considered all the elements of the neo-Keynesian system, we can return to the classical system of Chapter 3 to analyze the differences between the two. The tools we have developed along the way will help to make the comparison.

The major parts of the classical system are now considered inadequate. In part, the rejection is the result of changes in the world which have made the theory inapplicable, rather than actual errors in the theory. The nineteenth century was a period of rapid expansion in Western Europe and the United States. It was also the period in which modern banking was just developing. In such circumstances, there was a plentiful supply of investment opportunities; the problem was to choose between them and to find funds to finance those which were chosen. Such a period would tend toward full employment as its norm, with occasional but temporary lapses. It is therefore not surprising that economists tended to concentrate upon the problems of supply and efficiency: maximizing output from given capacity and increasing capacity by encouraging investment. Because it caused no problems, aggregate demand received little attention.

To examine the determination of the price level, remember that the classical theory visualized only one demand for money, the transactions demand. In such a case, the *LM* curve would be completely vertical at the income that would use the entire money supply for transactions. (This could be proved by deriving the *LM* curve using a liquidity function in which M_2 is zero at all rates of interest.)

Any change in M_s would cause a proportionate movement in the vertical *LM* curve. A change in the price level, by changing M_s, would cause a similar movement. (Notice that the classical theory of price changes worked through exactly the same mechanism as the Keynes effect. The different result occurred because there was no liquidity preference.)

If Keynes' only change had been to introduce liquidity preference, the classical system could have absorbed it. In fact, the basic idea had been introduced by dividing money into active and passive balances with different velocities. The revised quantity equation would then become

$$M_1V_1 + M_2V_2 = PY \tag{14.1}$$

where V_1 and V_2 are the respective velocities of the two demands for money. Then changes in price could often be explained as shifts from active to passive balances and back. Early business-cycle theories emphasized hoarding and dishoarding, which are alternative names for such shifts. In effect, the vertical *LM* curve was moving back and forth. Unfortunately, the classical system provided no systematic explanation for such shifts. The liquidity-preference function filled this gap by relating M_2 to the rate of interest. As such, it was within the spirit of the classical system.

One aspect, however, was not. This break is the *liquidity trap*. The possibility that the rate of interest might not fall low enough produced the possibility of a vertical portion of the demand curve. This led to what Keynes called a position of underemployment equilibrium. In one sense, Keynes was wrong. If supply exceeded demand, as shown in Figure 14.1, there could be no equilibrium. Prices and wages would continually fall as workers sought jobs and suppliers sought customers. In a more fundamental sense, Keynes was right, even though his choice of terms was unsatisfactory. Under the circumstances he envisioned, there would be unemployment and the falling wages and prices would do nothing to eliminate it. The society would be in permanent disequilibrium. We will return to this possibility shortly.

In the classical system, the division of national income between investment and consumption was believed to be determined by the interest rate. The demand for funds for investment was determined by productivity—what we have called the marginal efficiency of capi-

Underemployment "Equilibrium"

FIGURE 14.1

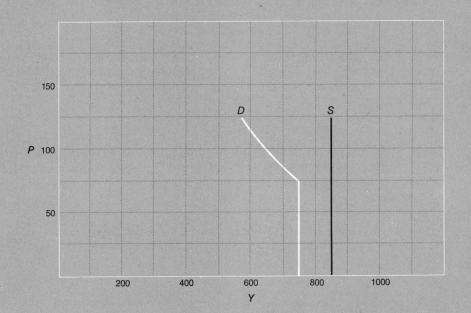

tal. The supply of funds came from saving. But what determines changes in saving? A concept such as the consumption function was useless, since income would be as high as it was possible to produce. If income did not change, one had to look at other factors to influence saving. Foremost among these was the rate of interest. In Chapter 6 it was mentioned that the rate of interest might have been an important determinant of saving at one time, even though it is no longer considered to be so. The intersection of the saving and investment schedules determined the rate of interest and the amount of saving and investment. This decision divides the national income between consumption and investment. This equilibrium is shown in graphic form in Figure 14.2.

Even this theory had within it the seeds of permanent disequilibrium. From what is now known about saving, it would be expected that the saving curve based upon full-employment income would intersect the horizontal axis at a positive level. It could therefore happen that saving and investment would not intersect at any positive rate of interest. In this case, the *IS* curve would intersect the axis as well. No amount of monetary expansion could produce full employment, for the interest rate would not be expected to become negative.

Once again the influence of the nineteenth century is very important. In that century, the investment-demand function was so great that the likelihood of its failing to intersect the saving function was very small. Only when an extended period of declining investment opportunity occurred (as it did in England in the 1920s and in the United States in the 1930s) did the possibility of a failure to intersect occur.

It is because of this possibility that the Pigou effect was so important. By introducing price changes into the *IS* curve, it rescued the classical system not only from the Keynesian *liquidity trap*, but also from the inherent possibilities which had always been implicit in the classical system itself but which had been prevented from occurring by the special character of investment demand. The Pigou effect also strengthened the belief in price and wage reductions as a device to combat depressions. If a fall in interest rates failed to bring about an adequate adjustment, a fall in prices and wages would finish the job.

It has sometimes been said that the Keynesian system depended upon rigid wage rates. The truth is slightly different. The Keynesian analysis demonstrated that flexible wages and prices were not a guarantee of full employment. Therefore the Keynesian system was developed so that it would be consistent with either rigid or flexible wages.

Classical Saving·Investment Equilibrium

FIGURE 14.2

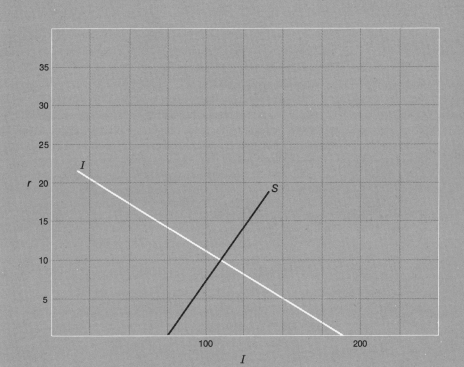

The classical system had no such versatility. When it found itself faced with a situation in which interest rates could not produce an equilibrium and in which wages and prices were too rigid for equilibrium, there was little more that could be said. The theory may have been sound, but it was irrelevant for the world.

Keynesian analysis could deal with rigid wages, and Keynesian policy tended to deemphasize wage changes. Keynes felt that lower wages might be useless and, if they were helpful, they were only doing a job which could be performed more easily by increasing the money supply. Accordingly, Keynes emphasized programs to increase demand, especially by shifting the *IS* curve.

It is the policy implications more than the analytical developments which indicate the psychological impact of Keynes upon economics. The possibility that price and wage changes would not eliminate unemployment destroyed the faith in the perfection of the economic system. If full employment was not automatic, government interference might be necessary. Around this possibility, great political arguments arose, studded with epithets. The argument has now subsided; the victory has gone to a synthesis based upon relevant parts of classical analysis, most of Keynesian analysis, and some factors that postdate both. In policy matters, the principle of government interference has been largely accepted, although wide areas of disagreement on particular policies remain. Some of these problems provide the basis for our next three chapters.

PROBLEMS AND DISCUSSION QUESTIONS

1. What are the classical and the Keynesian explanations of the effects of increased labor supply? Of an increase in the money supply? Of increased government spending?

2. Keynes called his analysis *The General Theory*. He said that the classical analysis was the special case of *The General Theory* at full employment. Do you agree?

3. Draw the *IS* and *LM* curves if there were no liquidity preference, but a low *MEC*. Does this produce underemployment equilibrum?

SUGGESTED ADDITIONAL READINGS

Discussions of Keynes and his predecessors are so numerous that only a modest selection can be given here. J. R. Hicks, "Mr. Keynes and the Classics," *Econometrica*,

(April 1937), reprinted in *Readings in the Theory of Income Distribution* (Homewood, Ill.: Richard D. Irwin, 1944), presents one widely held interpretation. *The New Economics*, Seymour E. Harris, ed. (New York: Knopf, 1950), contains several articles on the subject. Especially recommended are those by W. W. Leontief, R. F. Harrod, J. E. Meade, and Abba P. Lerner. Lawrence R. Klein discussed this relationship in Chapters 3, 4, and 5 of *The Keynesian Revolution* (New York: Macmillan, 1947). A. C. Pigou gives a somewhat rehabilitated version of the classical system in *Lapses from Full Employment* (London: Macmillan, 1945). Finally, Keynes himself emphasizes his differences from earlier theorists in *The General Theory of Employment, Interest and Money* (New York: Harcourt, 1936), especially in Chapter 2 and the Appendix to Chapter 19. Those attempting to read Keynes himself will find much help in Alvin Hansen, *Guide to Keynes* (New York: McGraw-Hill, 1953).

For a discussion of the particular role played by interest rates, *see* Lawrence S. Ritter, "The Role of Money in Keynesian Theory," in *Banking and Monetary Studies*, Deane Carson, ed. (Homewood, Ill.: Irwin, 1963).

The leading exponent of the "modern quantity" theory is Milton Friedman. See especially his "The Quantity Theory of Money—A Restatement," in *Studies in the Quantity Theory of Money* (Chicago, Ill.: University of Chicago Press, 1950). The other papers in this volume also deal with this subject.

The current phase of the controversy between classical and Keynesian economics usually centers upon the relative emphasis to be given to the multiplier and the velocity of money. *See especially* the discussion in *American Economic Review*, September 1965, featuring articles by A. Ando and F. Modigliani, M. DePrano and T. Mayer, and M. Friedman and D. Meiselman.

15

cApplied Governmental Policy

The purpose of this book has been to develop analytical tools for the study of national income and employment. Since tools are valuable only if they are used, this book should lead students to the discussion of questions of public policy. These next three chapters are intended to serve as a warning against hasty and incomplete applications of the principles presented in previous chapters. In these chapters, then, we shall discuss a few problems as examples of the kind of analysis required for policy decisions.

One should never lose sight of the limitations of any form of analysis. The discussion in this book has dealt only with the total figures for society and has ignored the changes that take place within these totals. For example, we have discussed only national income and have not considered the distribution of that income. Similarly, we have discussed taxes without considering the tax burden on individuals. Much of the public discussion accompanying any tax bill centers on these distributional aspects. Such discussion has a basis, both economic and ethical, not considered in this volume.

There is also an important limitation that is not inherent in the analysis, but that results from textbook presentation. Various factors have been considered one at a time; in practice they work together. The next two sections provide examples of such interrelations.

Government Spending and Taxes

Chapter 5 dealt with the relative effects of government spending and taxes upon national income. The analysis there discussed only the multipliers—that is, the reaction of consumption to the change in government activity. Later, in Chapter 7, it was noted that investment also is affected by government fiscal policy. In order to find the complete result of a change in government fiscal activities, it is necessary to combine the direct multiplier effects with the multiplier effects of the induced investment. In such a case, the total change in income is expressed by

$$\Delta Y = k_G \, \Delta G + k_I \, \Delta I \tag{15.1}$$

and

$$\Delta Y = k_{Tx} \, \Delta Tx + k_I \, \Delta I \tag{15.2}$$

Let us consider an example of such changes. If the marginal propensity to consume is $\frac{3}{5}$, what would be the effects of a change of $10 billion in government and in taxes? The simple multipliers indicate a change of $15 billion from the tax changes and $25 billion for the government spending.

It is quite possible that the change in investment which results from a tax change is more than that which results from government spending. The reason, of course, is that taxes have a disincentive effect, as potential taxes lower expected returns. For the purposes of this example, let us assume that each dollar of government spending increases investment by $10¢$, but that each dollar of tax cut increases investment by $60¢$. In this case, the total expansion from the increased government spending is $27.5 billion. Using Equation 15.1 and substituting values, we find that

$$\Delta Y = k_G \, \Delta G + k_I \, \Delta I \tag{15.1}$$
$$\Delta Y = (2.5 \times \$10) + (2.5 \times \$1)$$
$$= \$25 \qquad + \$2.5 \tag{15.3}$$
$$= \$27.5$$

Using Equation 15.2, we find that the expansion from a $10 billion-tax cut is $30 billion

$$\Delta Y = k_{Tx}\,\Delta Tx + k_I\,\Delta I \tag{15.2}$$

$$\Delta Y = (1.5 \times \$10) + (2.5 \times \$6)$$

$$= \$15 \qquad\quad + \$15 \tag{15.4}$$

$$= \$30$$

In such a circumstance, the balanced-budget multiplier might actually be negative—that is, a larger budget might mean a smaller national income. In the above example, an equal increase of taxes and government expenditures would actually have lowered national income by $2.5 billion.

We now see why the experience of the Cold War period does not help us to answer the question of stagnation. In Chapter 7 we mentioned that stagnationists argue that our high incomes have been dependent upon high government spending. Their opponents used arguments similar to that above to show that high government spending might actually have inhibited national income.

Like most economic problems that require a balancing of effects, this argument has no general solution, but only particular answers depending upon specific numbers. If a dollar of taxes destroyed only 40¢ worth of investment, the balanced-budget effect still would have been positive. We therefore must examine the special facts of particular cases.

In a depression, there is apt to be excess capacity in many lines of business. In such circumstances one should expect only slight changes in investment, and the total income effect would be only that shown by the direct multipliers. In periods of generally high-level activity, one might expect substantial investment reaction. For this reason, tax changes are usually considered good methods of fighting inflation and slight recessions, but government spending is more effective against a real depression.

An example of the use of taxes for this purpose was the general tax cut of 1963. This reduction, made at a time when employment was high but not full, was expected not only to stimulate the economy directly, but also to have significant effects upon investment. Indeed, most of the congressional discussion on the bill centered on the question of which taxes would do this job most effectively. This policy would probably have been pointless in a real depression, but as a stimulant to boost a healthy economy to even greater heights, it was quite appropriate. It will also be seen in Chapter 17 that the stimulation of investment has an important role in economic growth.

Monetary Aspects *of* Fiscal Policy

Another factor of substantial importance is the effect of government financing techniques on the money market. If the government finances its deficits by borrowing from individuals, the money supply is unchanged. (The sale of defense bonds or similar securities is an example of such a financing technique.) If the government should print money (a device seldom used in this country), the money supply increases by the amount of the deficit. The same effect would occur if the government borrowed from banks and the banks created deposits covered by excess reserves. If the government financed its deficits by selling bonds to the Federal Reserve System, the reserves of member banks would be increased by the amount of the deficit and the money supply could expand by a multiple of the increased reserves. If these expansionary methods of financing are chosen, one must make the appropriate changes in the *LM* curve, as well as in the *IS* curve. In general, a government deficit financed by bank borrowing is more expansionary than the same program financed by borrowing from individuals, unless the interest rate is already at the minimal level.

In Chapter 11 we observed that the multiplier effect must be adjusted to allow for changes in the money market. Figure 11.4 demonstrated that the increased income would require more money for transactions purposes, leaving less for liquidity and driving up interest rates. These higher interest rates would reduce investment, thereby reducing the impact of the increased government spending.

Such a result does not take place if the increased government spending creates an increase in the money supply. In this case, shifts in the *LM* curve keep interest rates from rising, or actually lower them. Such a shift is shown in Figure 15.1. In this case, an increase in the money supply equal to the increase in government spending actually lowers interest rates. The reason is that the velocity of money is greater than the multiplier. The increased money could, therefore, handle the transactions for more than the increased income generated by the government spending. The new equilibrium point is, consequently, just under $980 billion of income and just over 8 percent rate of interest, compared with $900 billion and 12 percent as shown in Figure 11.4, where only the *IS* shift was shown.

This example indicates why coordination between monetary and fiscal policy is important. If monetary authorities remain neutral, some of the expansionary effects of fiscal policy may be dissipated by higher interest rates and lowered investment. On the other hand,

Monetary Effect of Fiscal Policy

FIGURE 15.1

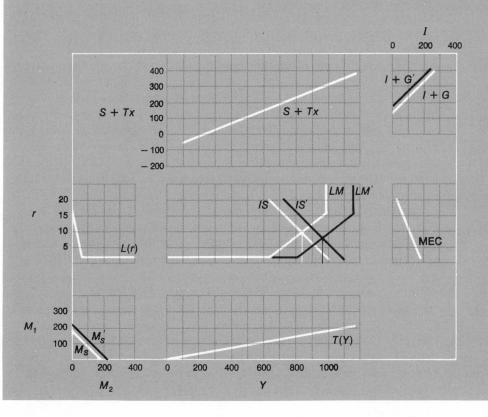

if both work together, monetary effects can be used to reinforce fiscal operations. Such coordination is easier in other countries where monetary and fiscal policy are both under the control of cabinet members. In the United States, fiscal operations are the primary responsibility of the Secretary of the Treasury, while monetary control is vested in the hands of the Federal Reserve Board, an independent agency. For this reason, the government occasionally seems to be following conflicting goals. That the system works at all is testimony that a fairly high degree of agreement can usually be effected.

Private Goods and Public Goods

In recent years, much discussion has been heard of public poverty amid private plenty. Many people have advocated building more and better roads, schools, and sewage systems and spending less on the gadgetry of private households. This has led many people to argue in favor of increased government spending for stabilization purposes.

Actually the two arguments are quite distinct and should be kept separate. Given the size of our capital stock, our population, and our technology, some maximum level of income can be produced. Out of that income, there is some mixture of private and public goods which would provide the highest level of consumer satisfaction. The problem of choice, on which the latter division depends, is based upon consumer preference, that all the tools of microeconomics help us to analyze. This book has been concerned with macroeconomics that discussed the development of the totals without regard to their composition. It is therefore improper to use one set of tools for answering another set of problems.

Actually, the argument that a certain government project *will provide jobs* is the poorest possible argument. Any equivalent government or private spending will provide jobs; the problem is to decide which job-producer will provide the greatest consumer satisfaction. This is a separate question to be argued on the merits of individual cases.

In general one would expect that private projects planned for long-run profit would have a substantial advantage over make-work government projects hastily developed to meet an unemployment emergency. Similarly, well-planned government works are probably better than private schemes designed mainly to secure a special subsidy or tax benefit. In other words, planning—whether private or public—takes time, and programs to help the country reach full employment should try to take full advantage of plans already made. However, even ill-planned projects are better than unemployment, for they use resources that would otherwise be wasted, produce some benefits directly, and effect substantial benefits through the multiplier. One might wish for full employment with a certain specific government share, but when these goals are in conflict full employment is apt to be preferable. Having achieved that goal, one can then try to improve the allocation between government and the private economy.

Scale and Timing

Additional problems are raised by the size of the coefficients in some of the functions and by the speed with which they take effect. If the multiplier is 10, it might be easy to persuade political leaders to restore full employment through government spending. In such a case, a gap of $50 billion would require $5 billion of additional spending. If the multiplier is nearer 2, it might be more difficult to persuade them to spend the required $25 billion.

Actually, the effective multiplier is nearer 2. Out of GNP must be subtracted depreciation, retained earnings, public and private social insurance contributions, and various taxes (all of which rise with GNP); and transfer payments, which move perversely, must be added. Thus the marginal ratio of disposable income to GNP is below $\frac{2}{3}$. The short-run marginal propensity to consume out of disposable income is approximately 0.8. Therefore, the effective marginal propensity to consume (the ratio of increased consumption to increased GNP) is about $\frac{1}{2}$, and the effective multiplier about 2. The tax multiplier is only about 1, which explains the emphasis upon incentives rather than upon the multiplier in the discussion of a major tax cut like that of 1963.

The low effective multiplier is testimony to the effectiveness of the automatic stabilizers in our economy. Not only are many government programs designed to have this stabilizing effect, but many private programs also do the same. The willingness of workers and unions to sacrifice possible wage increases in exchange for insurance and security programs leads in this direction, as do the dividend and depreciation policies of many firms. Consequently, the society has increased stability. Unfortunately, the stability persists even at undesirable levels, so that it is harder to get the economy moving out of a recession. On balance, the stability is probably good, but it is a mixed blessing.

Closely allied with the problem of scale is the problem of timing. How long would it take for any action to be effective? Could such action actually appear in time to do any good?

The answer depends upon what action is considered. Changes designed to increase investment might operate rather slowly, for investment planning takes time. The exception would be if the boost followed a previous tightening action, in which case there might be planned, but unexecuted, investments left over from the last action. In the other direction, restrictions on investment can take effect rather rapidly.

Actions that affect consumption can probably take effect rather rapidly, for many consumer purchases are either unplanned or the planning period is short. Therefore, consumption is apt to react rather rapidly to changes in disposable income. For the same reasons, the whole multiplier effect is apt to work its way out rather rapidly, although not instantaneously.

Like investment, large changes in government spending usually take time to become effective, for they require planning. The procurement practices of governments usually add even more time to the process. In addition, the political process of decision-making is not well adapted to rapid action except in extreme crisis. The 1963 tax cut was two years in the legislative process, and the tax increase proposed in 1967 was passed only in the summer of 1968.

Various proposals for speeding decision have been made. One suggestion was to give the president optional authority to adjust taxes or to start and stop government projects in accordance with the state of the economy. Another suggestion called for formula adjustments in tax rates in accordance with the level of employment. None of these suggestions made much progress, however, because congress has been unwilling to yield its control over fiscal matters.

Because of the delay in fiscal policy, many people have argued for greater reliance on monetary policy, which can be adjusted much more rapidly. Even so, the effects take time to work their way through the economy, particularly because monetary policy works primarily through investment.

All these problems of scale and time mean that government policy is still not a sufficiently flexible tool to guarantee stability. Certainly a major recession can be prevented; apart from that one must probably settle for less than perfection. Some economists speak of "fine-

The High-Employment Budget

FIGURE 15.2

Source: Federal Reserve Bank of St. Louis.

tuning the economy." Such a goal seems overly ambitious. The most practical program seems to be to use fiscal policy to achieve a suitable *average* level of income, apply automatic stabilizers to *dampen* fluctuations, and rely on the natural recuperative powers of the economy to do the rest.

The High-Employment Budget

The automatic character of many tax and transfer items has made the problem of planning for full employment somewhat more difficult. A tax adjustment that provided a modest government deficit at less than full employment, might become a government surplus at full employment. In order to avoid this problem, the President's Council of Economic Advisers introduced, in its 1962 report, a high-employment budget.

This budget indicates what the net federal surplus or deficit *would have been* if there had been full employment, not what it actually was at the existing level of economic activity. In this way, one can define a degree of "fiscal drag" which is independent of the actual level of the economy. Figure 15.2 shows this measure for recent years.

Because recent economic policy tends to aim at a suitable average level of income, rather than detailed reactions to every fluctuation, there is a need for measuring devices that concentrate on this over-all aspect. Current statistics tend to emphasize the details of the current economy. The increasing use of this new tool indicates increasing recognition of the inability to adjust for every change in the economy.

SUGGESTED ADDITIONAL READINGS

Problems of monetary and fiscal policy are matters of continuing concern to economists. The appropriate reading is, therefore, to be found in almost any issue of most economic journals, as well as the columns of daily newspapers. It is usually given special attention in the *Economic Report of the President* and the subsequent hearings and report of the Joint Economic Committee of the Congress.

16

Inflation

Although the basic tools of income analysis were developed in an atmosphere of unemployment and depression, they can also be applied to the analysis of problems of inflation. Before doing so, the meaning of inflation must be defined. In the discussion here, it will mean only rising prices. In some discussions, the term is confined to analysis of increases in the money supply. Although this may sometimes be a cause of inflation, it is not the only one; so it will be better here to reserve the name for the result and then discuss various causes.

Demand Pull

Probably the most common, and certainly the best-known, form of inflation arises from simple excessive demand. When for any reason there is an increase in demand, prices will tend to rise and output will tend to increase. If the society is already near full employment

Demand·Pull Inflation

FIGURE 16.1

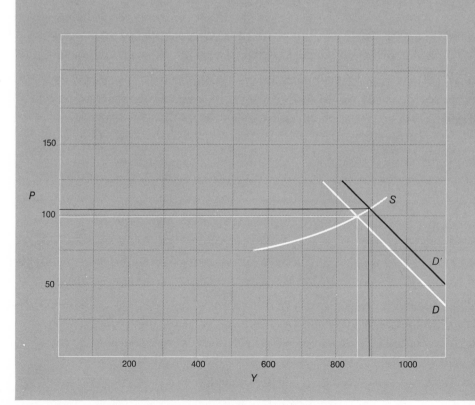

of men and capital, the effect of the increased demand will be mainly on price and only slightly on output. Such a situation is shown in Figure 16.1.

Demand-pull inflation occurs under many different circumstances. It occurs during cyclical booms when good times encourage high investment. Such investment, through the multiplier, creates an even larger shift in demand. It also occurs in wartime when the extraordinary level of government expenditures provides the trigger. It is common immediately after wars when pent-up consumption demand, released from the dual checks of patriotism and controls, provides the stimulus. (In this case it is often aggravated by a shift in supply to the left, as a result of wartime damage or conversion of facilities.) An inflationary situation may develop because the monetary authorities have permitted the creation of an excessive money supply. The resultant low interest rate would increase investment and income.

Against such inflation, all the standard tools to control demand can be used. In fiscal policy, decreased government spending and increased taxes are the obvious techniques. In monetary policy, all the devices that are used to lower the money supply are appropriate. Any action that will shift the *LM* curve or the *IS* curve to the left will lower effective demand and tend to cure the inflation.

Cost Push

A totally different form of inflation occurs from shifts in the supply curve. We have already mentioned the possibility of such a shift from the effects of war. More commonly, the supply curve shifts from increases in the money wage rate or an increase in the monopoly mark-up (see Figure 13.3). Such a shift leads to higher prices and *lower* output, as shown in Figure 16.2. Because the higher prices are usually accompanied by unemployment, this kind of case is sometimes referred to as an inflated recession.

Such inflation is probably a development of fairly recent origin. If there were monopolies in the society, we would expect them to have already increased their mark-up as much as would be profitable. Similarly, we would expect that if labor unions had the power to drive up money wages, they would have done so, stopping only at

Cost·Push Inflation

FIGURE 16.2

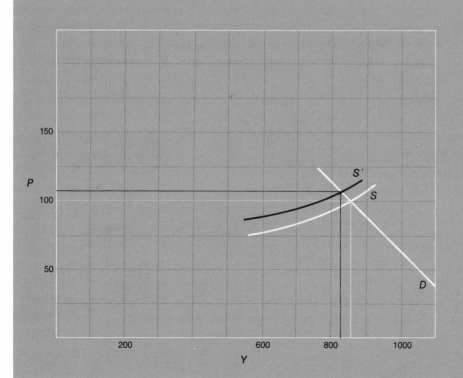

the point where higher wages would produce an unacceptable level of unemployment. If such power had been fully exploited in the past, there would be no remaining margin for shifting the supply curve without loss to those making the shift. Under these circumstances, the only cost-push inflationary pressure would arise from net increases in monopoly or union power, which are apt to be slight from year to year.

This line of reasoning has led many people to argue that cost-push inflation is an illusion. They have suggested that money wages and mark-ups will be increased only if there was a prior increase in demand. In that case, unions and monopolists are adjusting to a new situation that makes it possible for them to increase their demands without loss to themselves.

A new factor has appeared, however, in recent times. Those groups in the society who have special power are also very conspicuous. Important unions and major companies often do not wish to *exercise* all their potential power, for this would subject them to public criticism and possibly to direct government intervention. (The reaction of various governmental agencies to the proposed steel price increase in 1962 provided one such example.) When such public-relations motives are predominant there may be unexercised power. It is then possible for increases to come about at a time when no demand change has occurred. Such increases, however, tend to be the delayed result of previous increases in demand.

The results that are produced by such behavior create difficulties for public policy. When the initial increase in demand occurs the only observed effects are increased income and employment, both desirable. Later, when the price increases occur, they are accompanied by a decline in income and employment, both undesirable. At that stage, public policy to decrease demand would force prices back down, but only at the expense of still further decreases in employment. Since this effect is politically unpalatable, demand adjustment is not considered a suitable tool for use against cost-push inflation.

The usual tool that is used is government admonition, increasing the public pressure for stable wages and prices. Such action, however, does nothing to solve the problem. The unexploited opportunity remains, ready to create inflationary pressures any time an excuse can be found for an increase. For this reason, employers sometimes seem almost to welcome higher wage agreements, for these may give them an excuse to raise prices by more than the amount of the increase.

A new form of admonition was developed in the *Economic Report of the President* for 1965 and 1966, in the form of wage-price guidelines. These guidelines were based on the average gain in productivity in the economy of 3.6 percent per year. The Council of Economic Advisers proposed that average wages should increase at a rate of 3.6 percent per year, and average prices held steady. Industries whose productivity rose more than the average could actually lower prices, while industries with less increase could raise prices. Some additional wage adjustments were proposed for industries with changing demand for labor.

It is ironic that a tool so clearly adapted for dealing with cost-push inflation should have made its appearance in a time regarded by most economists as characterized by demand-pull inflation. Since little effort was made to control aggregate demand, the guidelines had little impact on the upward movement. The 1967 *Economic Report* tended to ignore the guidelines and the 1968 *Report* quietly buried them.

If the wage and price increases came together with the increase in demand, it would be possible to make more rational decisions about whether the output and employment gains were sufficient compensation for the price increases. If not, the usual tools could be used to lower demand and re-establish the old position. Instead, public-relations pressure separates the two and makes a unified judgment impossible. However, as a result of this situation, prices are on the average lower than they would be, held down by the fear of public criticism.

There does remain, however, one possible case of true cost-push inflation. Sometimes union leaders are sensitive to the wage bargains of other unions or are subject to special internal pressures in the union. Under such *political* pressure, union leaders can obtain wage increases that they would not seek if they were pure monopolists. Such increases could decrease employment so much that the gain in wage rates would not lead to a total increase in wages. Under these circumstances, one might witness cost-push inflation.

Bail Out

A special kind of inflationary pressure is sometimes created when the administration in power is especially sensitive to unemployment problems. A rise in the supply curve might occur, either because of unions or monopoly pressures. In the normal course of things, such a shift would lead to higher prices and lower employment. The admin-

ℬail·out Inflation

FIGURE 16.3

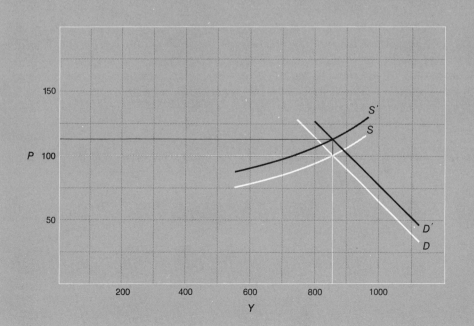

istration might seek to avoid unemployment by increasing demand. The ultimate solution, shown in Figure 16.3, would be higher wages and prices, but an unchanged level of real output.

When the administration is expected to act in this fashion, unions or monopolists might increase wages or mark-ups, knowing that such actions are unprofitable, but confident that the government will act so as to make them profitable. In such a case, it would be proper to say that both demand and supply are involved in the inflation, but the supply side may be the initiator.

In actual practice it may be difficult to distinguish this case from the previous ones. If wages rise and then prices, continuing alternately, it is hard to say whether unions initiate the increase and are then bailed out by the increase in demand, or whether the rise in demand makes it profitable to demand increased wages. In any case, it is clear that the process cannot continue without an increase in demand from some source.

The Choice of Policy Goals

In all of the above discussion, we have spoken as if there were a clearly defined goal of employment, output, and prices. Such is not the case. The problem is most obvious regarding employment.

At the end of 1967, 3.7 percent of the labor force was unemployed, and prices were rising at a rate of about 4 percent per year. Many people regarded this as a period of inflation and full employment. Nevertheless, many segments of the labor force were underutilized. Nonwhite workers had an unemployment rate of 7.4 percent, teen-agers a rate of 17.2 percent, and nonwhite teen-agers an unemployment rate of 26.4 percent. These figures suggest that even at this high level of economic activity, the economy was unable to provide jobs for those with lower skills.

We have seen that demand-pull inflation takes the economy up the supply curve to higher output, higher employment, and higher prices. As demand rises the value even of workers with low productivity becomes sufficiently high to justify employment. Should one attempt to stop the inflation, knowing that this is apt to eliminate jobs for the poorest members of our society? Alternatively, should one argue for even more inflation, as a reasonable price for helping those who need help the most? Which is the greater evil, inflation or unemployment? The choice is not an easy one to make, but it would be desirable to have a full awareness that it is indeed the choice that must be made.

A tool sometimes used to indicate the relationship between inflation and employment is the *Phillips curve*. This curve relates the *level* of unemployment to the *rate of change* in money wages. In the original work, calculated for the United Kingdom, it was found that money wages would remain stable only if unemployment averaged about 5½ percent. Product prices would remain stable at unemployment levels nearer 2½ percent.

In calculations for the United States, it is usually indicated that higher levels of unemployment would be associated with stable prices of wages. Whether the trade is worth the effort is a policy decision to be made. Economists can only point out the alternatives.

SUGGESTED ADDITIONAL READINGS

The literature of inflation is voluminous. As excellent collection of diverse points of view can be found in the staff papers and hearings of the Joint Economic Committee (86th Congress 1959–1960) under the general heading *Study of Employment, Growth and Price Levels.*

The Phillips curve made its first appearance in A. W. Phillips, "The Relation between Unemployment and the Rate of Change of Money Wage Rates in the United Kingdom, 1861–1957," *Economica,* vol. 25 (1958).

For a different approach, *see* E. Kuh, "A Productivity Theory of Wage Levels—An Alternative to the Phillips Curve," *The Review of Economic Studies,* vol. 34 (1967).

17

The Process *of* Economic Change

The chapters thus far have been limited to a study of comparative equilibrium positions, a kind of *before and after* study. In order to understand fully the operation of the economy, it is necessary to examine the process by which the economy moves from one position to another. Such study is called *dynamics*.

It has already been noted that one common characteristic of dynamic situations is that people make decisions on the basis of expectations of change. Investment is one form of economic activity which is especially dependent upon expectations. Consumption, too, often depends upon expected change, as when consumers stock up in expectation of rising prices or defer purchases in expectation of decreases. However, it is very difficult to discuss these matters systematically, because the basis on which these expectations are formed is questionable.

One characteristic of dynamic models is that they rapidly become very complex. This study, therefore, will be limited to an explanation of very simple models. These will serve as a sample of dynamic analysis.

$\mathcal{T}\!\!\mathit{he}$ Multiplier and the Accelerator

One easy way to make a theory dynamic is to assume that a certain time period is required for a reaction. The simplest such lag is to assume that a change in income in one time period produces a change in consumption only in the next. In Chapter 4, we worked through the multiplier process with such an assumption and saw that the level of income indicated by the multiplier will be approached only after a certain period of time.

We can add to our theory by combining it with the accelerator (Chapter 7). According to the accelerator principle, the amount of capital is proportional to the amount of consumption. Therefore

$$K_t = mC_t \qquad (17.1)$$

where K_t is the capital equipment required in year t, C_t is consumption and m is a constant. As consumption grows, required capital grows with it and investment is therefore required. This relationship is expressed in the following

$$
\begin{aligned}
I_t &= K_t - K_{t-1} \\
&= mC_t - mC_{t-1} \qquad (17.2) \\
&= m(C_t - C_{t-1})
\end{aligned}
$$

(We saw in Chapter 7 that there are reasons for believing that the accelerator is not an exact description of investment, but its basic idea is important enough to provide suggestive results.)

We can see how the multiplier pattern of Table 4.4 is modified by introducing the concept of the accelerator. This modification is shown in Table 17.1. We assume that there is, in addition to the investment induced by the accelerator, some exogenous investment— the result of government spending or of cost-lowering innovations. As before, we assume a marginal propensity to consume b of 0.6 and an accelerator coefficient m of 1.

This table shows a series of fluctuations about the \$250 level, eventually dying down and settling there at the income level determined by the multiplier.

It is interesting to observe that a cyclical pattern occurs even if the amount of exogenous investment varies from time to time. This

TABLE 17.1

ACCELERATOR-MULTIPLIER INTERACTION

Time	Exogenous Investment	Induced Investment	Consumption	Income
0	100	0	0	100.00
1	100	60.00	60.00	220.00
2	100	72.00	132.00	304.00
3	100	50.40	182.40	332.80
4	100	17.28	199.68	316.96
5	100	− 9.50	190.18	280.68
6	100	−21.77	168.41	246.64
7	100	−20.43	147.98	227.55
8	100	−11.45	136.53	225.08
9	100	− 1.48	135.05	233.57
10	100	5.09	140.14	245.23

is true whether the variation follows a pattern or is random in nature. (This statement can be checked by recalculating Table 17.1, using a series of random numbers for the exogenous investment. One might use the last two digits of telephone numbers from a page in the directory.)

It can be shown by a mathematical analysis of this problem that this damped cycle is not the only possible pattern, but occurs only when a particular relation exists between the accelerator coefficient and the marginal propensity to consume: between m and b. There are other possible patterns: a simple rise toward the multiplier value, as in Table 4.4; a cycle around it that explodes, rather than gradually diminishes, and a steady upward growth without any cycle. Table 17.2 illustrates each of these patterns.

The resulting incomes were calculated by the method used in Table 17.1, but with different values of b and m given for each pattern.

The simple accelerator-multiplier model is often used to explain shorter business cycles (cycles of about forty months) in our economy. Inventory changes, especially, which are among the chief characteristics of these business cycles, are thought to correspond rather closely to this picture of the accelerator.

TABLE 17.2

ALTERNATIVE ACCELERATOR-MULTIPLIER PATTERNS

Time	Simple Expansion	Exploding Cycle	Exploding Growth
	$b = 0.9$ $m = 0.5$	$b = 0.6$ $m = 2.0$	$b = 0.8$ $m = 3.0$
0	100.00	100.00	100.00
1	235.00	280.00	420.00
2	372.25	484.00	1204.00
3	496.80	635.20	2944.80
4	603.17	662.56	6633.76
5	690.72	530.38	14260.52
6	761.05	259.61	29812.65
7	816.60	− 69.15	61275.22
8	859.94	−336.01	124630.36
9	893.46	−421.85	251856.62
10	919.19	−256.11	506928.33

Continued Growth

A major goal of almost every society is continued growth. Its study is therefore as important as the study of fluctuations. One additional factor must be taken into account. So far we have assumed that production possibilities are fixed. Such an assumption is satisfactory for dealing with short-run problems, but is clearly inappropriate for long-run consideration. The investment that plays such an important role in today's demand will become a part of tomorrow's supply, for investment is merely another name for increases in capital.

By how much would income have to grow in order to provide full utilization of resources? Let us consider a very simplified case, without government, so that investment is the only offset to saving. Also, for simplicity's sake, we will assume that the marginal and average propensity to consume are equal. (These assumptions will merely simplify the algebra of this discussion; students who have come this far in the book should have no difficulty in adding these factors back in.) We would then have the following equations, similar to those of Chapter 4.

$$Y = C + I \tag{17.3}$$
$$C = bY \tag{17.4}$$
$$I = I_0 \tag{17.5}$$
$$S = Y - C \tag{17.6}$$

From these equations, we can easily calculate the level of investment:

$$I = S = (1 - b)Y \tag{17.7}$$

Since investment is the increase in capital, it is clear that the size of this increase will be $(1 - b)Y$. This extra capital can then produce an additional income. If the social productivity of new capital is represented by σ, then the possible increase in income can be represented by

$$\begin{aligned} \Delta Y &= \sigma \Delta K \\ &= \sigma I \\ &= \sigma(1 - b)Y \end{aligned} \tag{17.8}$$

Thus the potential rate of growth is the product of two ratios, the marginal propensity to save and the marginal social productivity of capital.

In an advanced society such as ours, the problem is that such a rate is so high that it is very difficult to maintain it. In particular the high level of saving, and the high productivity of investments may make such a rate very high. Accordingly, it may be necessary to raise consumption or expand government programs to provide a continuing boost to employment. (Notice that if investment is increased, it may solve the problem now but there will be an even bigger problem later.) The problem is to increase aggregate demand to keep pace with the growth in supply.

In underdeveloped countries, the problem is the opposite. Low incomes keep consumption so high that few resources are left over for saving. Even these resources often produce low increases in production, because the economic organization of the country is underdeveloped. In their case, the problem is to keep aggregate supply moving so as to provide for the potential demand.

The paradox of this situation is that rich countries must grow at a rapid rate in order to avoid depression, whereas poor countries can grow only at a very low rate.

It is not surprising that underdeveloped countries seek ways to increase their rate of growth. Government-saving programs, using taxation to obtain funds, and foreign borrowing are used to increase the flow of saving. In addition, various techniques have been developed to increase the effective value of σ, the social productivity of capital.

One important consideration is the direction of investment. Since some investments have a higher yield than others, it is important that funds be directed to those with the highest yields. Western countries rely on market processes for this direction, but many countries do not have such well-developed capital markets. Similarly, the entrepreneurial mentality, seeking profit wherever it may be, is quite widespread in our society. In underdeveloped countries, a more traditionalist attitude is more common. The problem of directing funds to those who will make the best use of them is therefore an important factor in increasing the productivity of capital.

Another important facet of the problem is the distinction between private and social productivity. It was already seen in Chapter 7 that some kinds of investment are often important in developing other opportunities. Such external effects mean that a particular investment might be socially useful even if it loses money, for it pays for itself through its impact on the profitability of other investments. Among the possibilities of these external effects are such traditional government activities of maintaining schools and roads and administering justice, but also private industries such as trade, finance, and transportation. Accordingly, subsidies to encourage their development are appropriate.

Thus, among the most important problems of developing economies are channeling funds to entrepreneurs and making allowances for external economies as a means of increasing the productivity of capital. Various programs for encouraging saving provide the other side of any development program.

Technology and Change

Although our major attention has been given to investment as the instrument of change, it is clear that changing technology has had a very profound impact on our own growth. Although it is not easy to separate the effects of technology and investment, it is probable that technology is at least as important as investment. However, the new technology is often embedded in new equipment so that the two go together.

Even though technological change is important in increasing our long-run income, its effects on employment are still feared. In the early days of the Industrial Revolution, workers smashed machines in their fear that the machines would supplant them in their jobs. Eventually, however, it became clear that technological improvement did not lead to permanent unemployment, for new jobs would be found for the displaced workers. Karl Marx created a new spectre, that of the "Reserve Army of the Unemployed." According to Marx, technological change always led to temporary unemployment, and before the displaced workers could be absorbed, new workers would be displaced by new machines. Thus, there would always be some members of society who were technologically unemployed.

In a superficial sense, Marx's view is correct. At any time, there are always some workers between jobs and therefore unemployed. Marx claimed more than this, however, for he felt that the reserve army kept wages down. For this to be true, it is necessary that the number of unemployed should exceed the number of unfilled jobs. We can apply the analysis of this volume in considering this problem. For simplicity, we assume that the supply of labor is fixed. The question then can be restated thus: If a society starts from a position of full employment, will technological improvement increase or decrease the amount of labor demanded? It is the demand for labor that affects the level of wages.

The analysis of this problem requires mainly the tools of aggregate supply. Technological change is represented by an upward shift of the production function. Ordinarily, such a shift also means a similar movement of the marginal productivity curve. The result of these changes is a new aggregate supply curve shown in Figure 17.1.

Figure 17.1 shows that at every level of prices more output is offered than previously. Similarly, no matter what the shape of the demand curve, the real income will rise. If the demand curve is relatively

Technological Progress and Unemployment

FIGURE 17.1

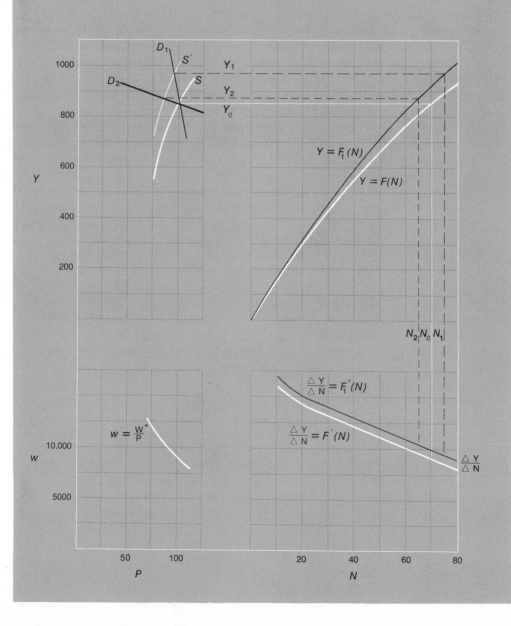

elastic like D_1, there will be a large change in output and slight change in prices. If the demand is inelastic like D_2, the change will be more in prices and less in output.

What of the demand for labor? Any given output can now be produced with less labor than before. Therefore a slight increase in output results in fewer jobs, and a large increase in output results in more jobs. Figure 17.1 shows this to be the case: with the elastic demand D_1, employment increases from N_0 to N_1; with the inelastic demand D_2, employment falls to N_2.

We could have arrived at the same conclusion from a consideration of price. With the new higher marginal product curve, employers would hire more workers at each real wage. However, the price decline associated with technological change has the effect of raising real wages. If the price change is small, the shift of the productivity curve will outweigh the rise in real wages; if the price change is large, the rise in wages will be more important.

Technological change can also shift the marginal efficiency of capital, usually upward. If so, the demand curve also shifts up, making an increase in employment more probable.

There is no absolute answer to the problem of technological unemployment. If the demand is elastic, the total number of jobs will increase and workers can be sure that anyone who loses his job will find another waiting for him. If demand is inelastic, technological change will require downward adjustment of money wages. In such a case, Marx would be right. Whether the aggregate demand will be elastic or inelastic will vary from country to country and time to time. Consumers and investors, by their preferences for lower prices or more goods, determine the effects of technology upon employment. When Marx announced the "Reserve Army" as a general law, he was quite wrong. Had he mentioned it as a possibility, he would have been correct.

SUGGESTED ADDITIONAL READINGS

The simple dynamic model is derived from Paul. A. Samuelson, "Interaction between the Multiplier Analysis and the Principle of Acceleration," *Review of Economic Statistics,* vol. 21 (1959), reprinted in *Readings in Business Cycle Theory* (Homewood, Ill.: Richard D. Irwin, Inc., 1944).

For models of long-run growth, *see* E. D. Domar, *Essays in the Theory of Economic Growth* (New York: Oxford, 1957); *and* R. F. Harrod, *Towards a Dynamic Economics* (London: Macmillan, 1949).

On the relation of technology to growth, *see* R. M. Solow, "Technical Change and the Aggregate Production Function," *Review of Economics and Statistics*, vol. 39 (1957).

Index

K

L

M

U

V

W